No Guarantee But God

No Guarantee But God

*The Story of the Founders of
OMS International*

by
EDWARD and ESTHER ERNY

Published by
OMS International
P.O. Box A
Greenwood, Indiana 46142

Second Printing, 1986
Third Printing, 2000

Reaching the nations for Christ

OMS International

Looking back on the 100-year history of OMS International, Inc., formerly the Oriental Missionary Society, our hearts are filled with praise and gratitude for the strong foundation upon which it was built.

Godly men and women, committed fully to obeying the Lord's every command, set us on a course relevant for today's needs of a lost world. Faith-filled founders spent hours in prayer seeking His plan and purpose. Thus, OMS' journey through the decades is linked to the legacy of holiness and the continuing chain of prayerful men and women who have heard His call and walked in obedience to the Great Commission.

As I read and reread the dramatic testimonies of our founders, Nakada, the Cowmans, and the Kilbournes, my heart is stirred. God renews my passion and burden for reaching the world with the Gospel. I pray that as you read their stories of full surrender, your life will also be challenged in a deeper commitment to carrying out the Great Commission.

Need we any guarantee but God?

J. B. Crouse, Jr.

J. B. Crouse, Jr.
President

Contents

Acknowledgments

Much of the material for this book has been drawn from early editions of OMS publications, *Electric Messages, The Missionary Standard,* and the biography of Charles Cowman, *Missionary Warrior,* written by his wife.

We are also indebted to Dr. B. H. Pearson for material obtained from his inspiring account of the life of Mrs. Cowman, *The Vision Lives.* The story of Juji Nakada could not have been written apart from the help of Arthur Shelton who researched Rev. Nakada's life story for an article published in the missionary journal, *Japan Harvest.* For the chapter on Ernest Kilbourne, we borrowed generously from a manuscript prepared by his son, E. L. Kilbourne, a missionary himself with a distinguished record of service in Japan, Korea, and China.

Preface

Psychologists agree that modern man's most basic need is security. This need urges him on in a relentless search for better ways to fortify himself against a hostile world and the vicissitudes of life. Inasmuch as it is humanly possible the future must be robbed of its uncertainties through the promise of unemployment compensation, a guaranteed annual wage, a 50,000-mile automobile warranty.

This is a book about men who thought of security in essentially different terms. Such men the world has always regarded with knowing smiles and quickly dismissed as visionary hopelessly impractical I I crackpots. "

As far back as Abraham, there have been such men (though their numbers have always been few)-who were content to leave all that was familiar, going out "not knowing whither"; men who forsook kingdoms and endured hardships "seeing Him who is invisible"; men glad to leave earthly hometowns in search of "a city which hath foundations, whose builder and maker is God." Not knowing "whither" or "from whence," they knew "Whom" and they were confident that in this life that was all they needed to know. This was to them ultimate security. Beyond this they needed no guarantee but God.

Such were Charles and Lettie Cowman, Juji Nakada, and Ernest Kilbourne. Their faith fashioned the organization that is today OMS International. For a century God has been pleased to use it as an instrument to bring multitudes in many lands to a knowledge of Himself. The first four chapters detail God's working in the lives of OMS' founders. The epilogue provides a record of the ministries of OMS International at the present time.

1

Charles Cowman

Charles Cowman never forgot the night it happened. It was only to satisfy his wife that he had agreed to attend the revival services at Chicago's Grace Methodist Church. He could appreciate the religious training of his youth, but as he patiently explained to his wife, "One cannot live a Christian life in a telegraph office."

The simple service—the once-familiar songs, the sincere testimonies—had an unexpected effect on the handsome young telegrapher. "Suddenly there came into my heart," he recalled, "a deep, unutterable yearning to make the experience my own. A battle raged...how truly I had reached the place of Calvary."

"After the service we started home," Cowman later wrote of that night, "and being under deep conviction I could not utter a word, but broke out in sobs. We walked twelve blocks and hastily entered our apartment and, without taking time to turn on the lights, we knelt by a chair and there I poured out my confession to God, asking Him to take back the prodigal."

That night, by the altar in his home, a fire was kindled in the heart of Charles Cowman that would take him from Chicago to Japan in a ceaseless search for lost men. This was a passion that would one day be translated into an organization destined to plant the gospel of Jesus Christ in millions of homes and bring the soul-transforming message to multitudes of waiting hearts.

Many years before that unforgettable night in Chicago, the hand of

1

God had been at work in the life of Charles Cowman, preparing for Himself a chosen instrument.

Charles' parents, David and Mary Cowman, were of pioneer stock. They moved from Illinois to Iowa in 1870, bought a farm, and established a home. The Cowman homestead became a favorite stopping place for the roving circuit riders, and religion was administered in healthy doses by father Cowman, a man described as "the very soul of honor and one who expected as much from everybody else."

The daily readings from the thumb-worn family Bible left an indelible impression upon the mind of the small boy.

Sunday was "The Lord's Day" in the Cowman home and was treated accordingly. Even sub-zero weather was no excuse for failure to attend the small Methodist chapel where the family held its membership.

Life on the frontier was strenuous. There were few luxuries and long hours left little time for leisure. But these years added to the character of Charles Cowman priceless ingredients—rugged honesty, quiet courage, and a genuine love for hard work.

The lad soon distinguished himself as a natural leader. He also demonstrated a rare sensibility and tenderness toward the things of God. One night during the concluding service of a revival meeting, Charles, without persuasion, left his seat and walked down to the mourners' bench. There he knelt, sobbing in penitence. The revival meeting, however, was pronounced a failure by many in the community. Only one small boy had found Christ.

While in his teens, Charles developed a close friendship with a young telegraph operator in a nearby town. His quick mind was intrigued by the magic of telegraphy, and the clatter of messages leaping from deft fingers onto the wire became an increasing fascination. Soon he was spending many hours in the telegraph office. Charles had no intention of making telegraphy his life work, but with his growing skills as an operator came the offer of a position. Reluctantly, his parents gave their consent and the fifteen-year-old left home to take a man's job.

The lad's exceptional abilities were immediately recognized by his superiors. He was referred to with some awe as "the boy operator." One promotion followed another. By his seventeenth birthday he was chief dispatcher at one of the largest divisional centers on the Burlington Railway. By nineteen he was in Chicago filling a responsible post with the same company and drawing an unusually large salary for a mere boy.

At the age of 21 he married his childhood sweetheart, Lettie Burd. She was a cultured young woman who had once considered a career in opera. Their first home was in Glenwood Springs, Colorado, where Charles had moved to escape the harsh surroundings of the big city. During the years away from home, he had drifted from his early religious moorings. His work kept him at his desk on Sundays. Church attendance was neglected, and the voice of God seemed to have died out in his soul.

Charles Cowman now sensed little need for God. Possessed with remarkable energies and endowed with conspicuous gifts, he was the picture of success. And to this success was added the joy of his marriage.

"Our childhood dream was realized," said Lettie. "It seemed for us that heaven had begun; but God, whose ways are higher than our ways, had to stir up that cozy nest—that His purpose for the future might be carried out."

The altitude proved too high for Mrs. Cowman. One night when it appeared that her life would flicker out, Charles fell by her bed and cried, "Oh, God, spare her life. Remember the boy who used to pray. If you'll only spare her I'll serve you all my life." It was a prayer Charles was to remember later.

Lettie Cowman recovered, but the doctor advised an immediate change of climate. Soon the Cowmans were back in Chicago where Charles was made chief of the New York division of the Western Union office—a responsible post with 300 operators under him. With this advance came increased affluence. The prayer he had prayed by the bedside of his dying wife was forgotten. "I had drifted away from God and my earliest religious training," Cowman later wrote. "After our marriage we were thrown into a worldly society and continued there until 1892."

One night shortly before Christmas of that year, a Christian worker called at the Cowman home inviting them to a special meeting in one of the neighborhood churches. The invitation would have been accorded a polite refusal but for one unusual fact—the speaker was a converted opera singer. That night Lettie Cowman was in church.

The meeting, as it turned out, was a children's service. The opera singer told very simply how she had one day asked the Good Shepherd to come into her heart. Then she sang:

> There were ninety and nine that safely lay
> In the shelter of the fold;
> But one was out on the hills away
> Far off from the streets of gold.

"It was like the singing of Paul and Silas in the jail," Charles later wrote of the event, "and it was accompanied by a spiritual earthquake." At the invitation, Lettie Cowman knelt amid a cluster of small children at the altar rail to give her heart to Christ.

"The change in my wife which followed was a great surprise to me," said Charles, "for she at once separated herself from the world and testified that she was genuinely converted. She began dealing with me, but I told her that living a Christian life in a telegraph office was an impossibility."

Lettie joined the Grace Methodist Church and began a war of intercession for the soul of her husband. Finally one night he agreed to accompany her to a revival meeting.

"As I sat there in the meeting," Cowman described, "there arose out of the misty past a vision of an old mourners' bench and the revival scenes out in the dear open county...but uppermost in my mind was the time when the life of my loved one had been spared through my humble prayer. What of that unfulfilled vow?"

When the invitation was given, Lettie asked Charles to go with her to the altar. But he refused with a terse, "Not tonight."

The evangelist then urged the Christians to come forward to pray. Lettie left her husband and walked slowly down the long aisle. As Charles watched, it seemed to him that a great gulf was widening between him and his beloved wife. "That of itself almost broke my heart," he said, "for we were rare lovers and I would have readily laid down my life for her."

But the Holy Spirit of God now relentlessly pursued the soul of the young telegraph executive. After the service, Charles stumbled home in an agony of conviction. All resistance gone, he fell by a chair to weep his way back to God.

"From that point on Charles Cowman made it the first thing in his life to be a Christian," his wife afterwards wrote. "For thirty-six years amidst all the testings and buffetings it held him as firm as the Rock of Ages.''

A few days later Cowman went to his office determined to win a soul to Christ. In one corner of the long room sat a man at his desk who apparently had a few minutes to spare. Back and forth Cowman walked summoning courage to speak to him. Finally an effort was made. For a half hour he stood beside the desk engaged in a one-sided conversation.

Cowman left the office that night convinced that his first effort at soul-winning had been a total failure.

The next day when he returned to the job the young man to whom he had witnessed was waiting for him. ''I went home last night after our conversation,'' he explained excitedly, ''and I did just what you told me. It's all settled. I have given myself to Christ.''

Charles Cowman could hardly have known that his first convert, Ernest A. Kilbourne, would one day be his fellow missionary and closest friend. That day a lifelong partnership was begun which fused two souls into an intimate spiritual brotherhood to be broken only by death.

Charles Cowman was a skilled winner of souls. What he lacked in training he made up for in compelling love and sympathetic understanding that broke down all resistance. In less than six months he had personally led 75 of his fellow workers to the Lord. When asked about the secret of soul-winning he would exclaim, ''How shall we do personal work? Just begin and do it and let the method unfold itself.''

''He was a tireless personal worker,'' one of Cowman's associates testified. ''There were some 500 men working in the office and he tried to see and talk with every one of them about his soul's welfare ...he was always buying up opportunities, redeeming the time. He was a good salesman; he did not leave the case with closed doors, but always with a way to return and talk about it some more.''

The work hours kept many telegraphers from attending church services, so Cowman devised a plan for nourishing the growing band of converts. The parlor of a nearby hotel was secured for an hour on Sunday afternoon and there services were held.

The fellowship became known as the Telegraphers Band. ''Why not reach telegraphers in other cities and towns,'' Cowman suggested. Operators in offices throughout the United States and Great

Britain were contacted and many of them won to Christ.

One of Cowman's associates who recalled the first small meetings of the Telegraphers Band said, "I have often thought of this as the beginning of The Oriental Missionary Society."

Soon Charles Cowman's passion for lost men was moving him beyond the telegraph office to other parishes. The vilest section of Chicago was then known as "Little Hell." It was a sort of human garbage dump frequented by desperate and forgotten men. In the Little Hell mission hall, Cowman preached his first sermon.

For a week in advance he prepared for the message. Hours were spent on his knees before the open Word. The evening he was to preach he walked the mile and a half to the mission in prayerful silence. When he finally stood to speak he was shaken by the tragic picture before him—a sea of faces reflecting with awful eloquence the ravages of sin. The carefully prepared message was forgotten. Where words failed to win, his tears succeeded. That night they came—a long altar full of them. In an instant Cowman was down on his knees among them. And there he remained till midnight, praying with the last seeker. Thereafter, Sunday evenings found him with the derelicts in Little Hell. "That was my missionary training college," he later told a friend.

Charles Cowman had been a Christian one full year when an incident occurred that was to alter forever his life and ministry. At work in the telegraph office one night, the quiet self-possessed man became impatient and spoke harshly to one of his subordinates. Quickly he recovered, asking the operator's forgiveness; but the outburst provided a flash of insight that left his sensitive soul troubled. For help he turned to an earnest Christian, George Simister, a leading layman in the church where the Cowmans attended.

Simister had frequently spoken to Cowman about a deeper experience which he called "sanctification" or the "filling of the Spirit." This life, he explained, was marked by a complete purity of heart.

"Brother Cowman, you need to have your heart cleansed from all sin," was Simister's diagnosis after Cowman had described his outburst of temper. Thus began the telegrapher's quest for the fullness of the Holy Spirit—a quest that soon resulted in what he forever termed "a second work of grace."

"I have committed myself and my all into God's hands," wrote

Cowman on the day of this experience. "He has accepted the offering. Life can henceforth never be the same."

"New power marked his service from that day," said his wife. "He was truly sanctified and holiness had in him not only an advocate but an illustration...his life was one simple, long fulfillment of the will of God as he understood it."

So real was this new life to Charles Cowman that he felt compelled to urge others to enter into the blessing. This conviction, a prime emphasis throughout his ministry, would leave its indelible imprint on The Oriental Missionary Society.

In Japan, Cowman wrote, "Young and old converts are hungering and thirsting for the blessing of full salvation...more and more I am realizing that we should strongly emphasize the need of being filled with the Holy Spirit. This is the secret of successful soul-winning."

From this point on, Charles Cowman's life was filled with incessant activity for his Lord. When confronted by need, he could not resist the urge to do something—to act. With the vision of Christian stewardship came characteristic action. He organized a tithers' league in his own church and boldly denounced fairs and festivals as means of raising money for the Lord's work. He kept scrupulous account of all money that passed through his hands. The well-furnished home he exchanged for a small apartment in order to support another worker in Africa. "How can you afford to support so many native workers?" a friend inquired. "I can't afford it," came the reply. "I sacrifice it."

Cowman's work in the Little Hell mission inspired him to begin a mission of his own. He rented a storeroom with a basement below, equipped it with benches and beds, and invited drunks and gamblers to spend the night there on the condition that they attend his preaching service.

"Hundreds of men were reached in that way," said a friend. "He had a way with those men. He disarmed them by trusting them."

Invitations began to come from pastors of the largest churches in the city, urging Cowman to relate his experiences of soul-winning in an unusual parish—a telegraph office. His messages were brief and usually took the form of a simple testimony.

One invitation came from a Chicago pastor, noted for his pulpit oratory. After the service he asked Cowman to come to his study. "I try to win souls but fail every time," he confessed. "Can you tell me the reason?''

It was three o'clock in the morning when the two men emerged from the study, faces shining. By the following Sunday the word was being whispered from pew to pew. ''What is it? Something's happened to our pastor!''

Within a few weeks the church was experiencing a great revival. During a service in which the Cowmans were present, the minister came down from the pulpit, slipped his arm about the young telegrapher and said, ''God bless you, Brother Cowman, for your faithfulness to me that night. I would rather have the love of God shed abroad in my heart and witness the scenes of the past two weeks than to have the world at my feet.''

As increasing opportunities for service presented themselves, Charles Cowman became acutely conscious of his need for Bible training. His shift in the telegraph office kept him busy from 5 p.m. until midnight. This permitted him to enroll for half-day sessions at the Moody Bible Institute. He kept to this rigorous schedule for six years until his work at the institute was completed.

Shortly before the turn of the century, a great missionary convention was held at the Moody Bible Church—a convention that was to play a key role in the making of the young missionary, Charles Cowman. Noted missionaries from every continent were present. Dr. A. B. Simpson, founder of The Christian and Missionary Alliance, was the principal speaker.

In his message Simpson told of a young businessman who with his wife and small child had gone into the heart of Africa, trusting in God to supply their needs. The message got through. This kind of self-denial found a response in the heart of the executive from Western Union.

Cowman, as a matter of principle, never did things by halves. When the offering was taken, he pulled out a wad of bills—a full month's salary—and placed it in the collection plate along with his gold watch.

But Charles Cowman was not through giving. After the offering, Simpson made another appeal: ''If there are any young people here who will offer themselves as missionaries providing God calls,'' he challenged, ''stand up, right where you are.''

Cowman turned to his wife. ''This means you and me,'' he said.

In a moment both of them were on their feet.

It was the vast, subcontinent of India to which the hearts of Charles and Lettie were first drawn. But the door to India was closed to them when Mrs. Cowman failed to pass the medical examination required of all new candidates.

Amidst this frustration God sent Arthur T. Pierson, an experienced Christian statesman, with wise words of counsel: "Wait, young man, wait God's hour. " So Charles and Lettie Cowman waited; and they prayed.

A casual meeting one Sunday morning at the Grace Methodist Church provided another link in the chain of circumstances through which God was moving Charles Cowman toward the Orient. The service had just begun when a young Japanese walked down the aisle, seating himself directly in front of Charles. His features were striking and his eyes smouldered with the intensity of purpose that marks a man for leadership. His name was Juji Nakada.

"I came to America to get filled with the Holy Spirit," Nakada explained to Cowman when they met after the service. Thus began a friendship that drew like minds together in common purpose that would find dynamic expression in The Oriental Missionary Society.

The Telegraphers Mission Band pledged to support Juji Nakada, sending him back to Japan as their representative. From Japan, Nakada wrote Cowman of his evangelistic work. These reports fired the telegrapher's imagination and gripped his heart with the plight of 57 million souls waiting for the life-giving message.

On a blank page in Charles Cowman's Bible we find the following brief entry: "Called to Japan. August 11, 1900, 10:30 a.m." This was to prove a signal day in his life. The call had not come in a stirring service nor following an emotional appeal. Like Elijah of old, he had received the message in a "still small voice." Alone that Sunday morning in the quiet of his study he had heard God speak unmistakably. So certain was the call that it bore him unfalteringly through the years of hardship and suffering that were to follow.

When Lettie returned from church that morning Charles met her at the door, his face streaked with tears. Taking her by the hand, he led the way to the study where he opened his Bible to Matthew 20:4 and read, "Go ye into the vineyard and whatsoever is right I will give you." Turning to his wife he said, "God wants us in Japan."

Her reply provides a remarkable illustration of divine guidance. "Six weeks ago, while I was alone," she said, "God spoke to me about going to Japan. I have been waiting the right moment to tell you."

Charles Cowman's days in the telegraph office were at an end. Now the offer of a more lucrative position held no appeal. "Had he remained with the company," said a Western Union official, "he would have been one of the leading men in the telegraph service. He has, however, chosen that which is permanent and lasting."

The Cowmans first applied to the Methodist Mission Board for service in Japan and in a short time were under appointment. Charles was to teach English in a mission school and Lettie was to be professor of music. Once the decision was made, however, Charles was seized by a growing uneasiness that finally drove him to his knees in quiet desperation. Soon the issue was settled. Connections with the Methodist Missionary Society were severed and Charles announced the plan God had shown him. "God wants us to go to Japan trusting Him alone and independent of any established missionary organization," he explained.

Evidences that this plan was indeed of God quickly followed. The next Sunday a woman slipped a dollar into Cowman's hand. "This is for your work in Japan," she told him. From an unexpected source $300 came designated "For steamer fares to Japan." In another service a gentleman gave Cowman a check for $240, saying, "Please accept this for the first year's rent on your proposed Bible training school." The Telegraphers Band agreed to send the Cowmans their offerings from time to time; but aside from this tentative promise, the new missionaries had no guarantee but God.

On the first morning in February 1901, a small group of friends, among them a number of telegraph operators, gathered on a pier at San Francisco to farewell Charles and Lettie Cowman.

From the boat Cowman waved to his friends on the shore and sang:

> I do not ask to see the way
> My feet shall have to tread
> But only that my soul may feast
> Upon the Living Bread.

At noon the gangplank was lifted and the ship slipped away from the dock, her bow set in the direction of the "Land of the Rising

Sun."

In his cabin, Cowman wrote in his diary, "One is walking by our side whose smile is as gentle as the breath of evening...unseen hosts are marching by our side. Invisible armies are filling the air. We expect great and mighty things to come to pass."

Twenty-one days later they watched a rockbound coastline emerge from a shroud of gray mist. Before them lay the port city of Yokohama and Japan. On the dock stood the evangelist Juji Nakada; he had come to welcome his friend from Chicago. For the two men the day marked the fulfillment of a dream and the beginning of an enterprise for which multitudes would one day thank God.

"Tokyo, Japan, February 22, 1901. A new era in our lives," wrote Cowman the day of his arrival. "Oh, for faith, unyielding faith!" The plea was an appropriate one. The coming months would present the new missionaries with ample opportunity to prove the God to whom they had so recklessly abandoned themselves.

Even in 1901 Tokyo was a great congested city with a population of nearly 3 million. Missionaries generally considered the turbulent heart of Tokyo unfit for residence and situated in the more tenable areas near the suburbs.

The Cowmans could afford no such luxury; nor would they have chosen it. Instead, they rented a two-story building in the Jimbo-Cho district near the conflux of busy thoroughfares in the heart of Tokyo. The downstairs served as the gospel hall; above were rooms for students, adjacent to the Cowmans' living quarters.

"I wish you could see us in our new home," Charles wrote a friend in Chicago. "The building we rented had been used as a children's school and tots had scrawled Chinese characters all over the walls; it was a sight to behold...there was nothing to do but paint it. I searched through every shop in the neighborhood for paint but could find nothing but red—a bright red. Now imagine your bedroom and kitchen walls a flaming red.

"We were able to furnish our home for about $20.00. Extravagance! In our front room we have a straw matting, two straightbacked chairs, and a bamboo center table. In the bedroom, where is the bed? We searched every secondhand store for a bed, but could find none, so we did the next best thing—made a mattress of bamboo leaves. We feel rich and thank God every day for permitting us to be here. The center of God's will is our home.''

At night the Cowmans discovered that they were sharing their quarters with uninvited guests. ''I do not fancy you would enjoy spending the night with us,'' Cowman wrote. ''Rats (small and large rats) turn handsprings over our bed. For a change they hold high carnival, racing around the room and over the ceiling until frightened away.''

When guests dropped in, the new missionaries offered no apologies for their small home and meager fare. Once when a noted author visited them, ten cents was all the money they possessed. The larder was reduced to half a loaf of bread and a bit of tea. Mrs. Cowman, however, covered the table as usual with a dainty white cloth; on it she placed the half loaf of bread and cups of tea. Her husband sat at the head of the table ''with as much dignity,'' she recalled, ''as if he had been presiding at a banquet.''

''What did you do?'' Cowman was later asked when he related the experience.

''There was nothing left for us to do,'' he replied, ''but to pray, 'Give us this day our daily bread.' And this my good wife and I did with all the earnestness we could command.''

If visitors were sometimes surprised by the simplicity of their fare, they were even more impressed by the simplicity of their faith. A lady visitor from a well-known college once inquired, ''Where are your diplomas and your credentials, Mr. Cowman?'' He answered that his college of missions had been the telegraph office in Chicago and his credentials—all that he possessed—were found in II Cor. 6:4-10.

A constant companion during these early years in Japan was a slim volume of the *Diary of David Brainerd,* pioneer missionary to the American Indians. The following words Cowman had heavily underscored: ''I cared not where or how I lived, or what hardship I went through so that I could gain souls for Christ. While I was asleep I dreamed of these things, and when I wakened the first thing I thought of was this great work.''

To properly evaluate the contribution of Charles Cowman, he must be observed against the backdrop of his own times. The early twentieth century was marked by a prevailing spirit of colonialism that influenced all relationships between the United States, Great Britain, and the so-called ''backward'' nations; nor was missionary enterprise untouched by the ''paternalism'' that this policy engendered.

Missionaries frequently thought of themselves as "great white shepherds" commissioned to make foreign converts and superintend the flock. They alone were judged capable of pastoring the churches, evangelizing, and dispensing funds. Nationals were commonly regarded as "precious souls" but woefully ignorant, irresponsible, and completely incapable of self-government.

In light of these facts, it is not difficult to understand why Cowman's methods were not always fully appreciated by other missionaries. After witnessing the effectiveness of his fiery young co-worker, Juji Nakada, Cowman came to the following conclusion: "The task of the missionary," he insisted, "is to train the national to pastor and evangelize his own people." In short, Charles Cowman believed that the native church should be entirely indigenous—self-supporting, self-governing, and self-propagating. The missionary's task: to remain in the background and make himself dispensable as quickly as possible. The objective of the infant missionary society, he determined, would henceforth be to train nationals to win their own people. Like Moses on Sinai, Cowman was convinced that this was the pattern God had given for the building. Sixty years and the devastation of a world war were to prove the wisdom of the plan.

The Bible training institute headed by Cowman and Nakada became a spiritual boot camp that was soon turning out young Japanese evangelists, effectively afire with a zeal communicated directly from the heart of their leaders. These were not classical scholars. Often unfamiliar with the fine points of theology, they were nonetheless steeped in Bible and able to handle their mother tongue convincingly. More important, they were Spirit-filled young men who had caught the vision of the value of a soul.

The Bible institute doubled as an evangelistic hall. A signboard above the narrow entrance announced in large characters:

> Jesus Doctrine Mission Hall
> Services Every Night
> Everyone Welcome

Night after night they came, jostling their way through the narrow doors to fill every seat and crowd the window spaces. Nakada was usually the preacher. Following a stirring message he would urge seekers to come to the front and kneel at the long wooden altar. They came. During the next ten years 15,000 found Christ in the Jimbo Cho hall alone. One after another, additional halls were opened, and these became the cradle of the young church.

The first hall had been open less than a week when Cowman had an opportunity to win his first Japanese convert. Nakada had given the invitation and the response was so overwhelming that he found himself short of personal workers. Discovering a seeker who knew a bit of English, he beckoned to Cowman (whose knowledge of Japanese was still very limited). By a remarkable coincidence, the young seeker turned out to be a telegrapher in Tokyo's Central Telegraph office. Cowman's joy was unbounded. Soundly converted, the young operator became an unflagging witness to his new faith. Within a week he had brought six fellow telegraphers to Christ.

From the simple beginning in a single hall in the bosom of a vast city, the work of God began its relentless growth, reaching out toward the furthermost corner of the islands. Wherever the gospel went, Cowman encountered an appalling spiritual hunger—a hunger that never failed to stir him.

"Today I had the privilege of preaching through an interpreter in an open-air meeting," he wrote to a friend. "It was not a congregation or an assembly nor a crowd, but a tremendous torrent of human beings. . .we began at 2:30 p.m. and kept right on for hours. I spoke until my soul and body were nearly bidding each other farewell. . .I felt there were multitudes who will never, never worship idols again."

One of the largest auditoriums in Tokyo was rented for special services. The doors had scarcely opened when, as Cowman described, "fifteen hundred people rushed in. Never before have I witnessed such meetings. . .It is a time of great revival and Tokyo is being moved by the power of the Holy Ghost."

As the work grew, Cowman appealed for missionaries to join him. His close friend and colleague, E. A. Kilbourne, who had been heading up the Telegraphers Band, was the first to arrive. For a time the mission was known as the Cowman-Kilbourne work, but continued growth required that it be officially named and carefully organized. The Oriental Missionary Society was the name the two men chose. Publication of a small magazine titled *Electric Messages* was begun. This, the forerunner of *The Missionary Standard,* described in glowing reports the growth of the mission to an ever-increasing constituency in the homeland.

From Tokyo Cowman and Kilbourne made numerous evangelistic tours—trips that took them inland into hitherto unreached villages. Everywhere they encountered open hearts. An innkeeper touched by the signing of a gospel song said, "Please, won't you sing that song again?" The next morning he was up before dawn to tell them, "Last night I prayed to your God and peace came to my heart." After one evangelistic service an old woman responded with an unforgettable statement: "I always knew that there ought to be a God like that."

Within 23 years 201 mission stations and an equal number of itinerary points were opened. Believers were organized into congregations and a new Bible school erected for the training of Japanese pastors and evangelists.

The church's annual conferences were times of virtual Pentecost. Cowman describes one such occasion:

"At the opening meeting prayer was outpoured for several hours and we heard one continuous stream of intercession. Everybody prayed quite oblivious to one another, when suddenly there came a hush like the receding of an ocean wave.

"Three full days were spent in waiting on God before these meetings. Far off in the quiet country, in an abandoned farm house, the native workers waited and prayed until all felt that God had heard them, and then returned with faces shining as if they had been on the Mount of Transfiguration."

For decades missionaries had concentrated their efforts in the cities of Japan. But the majority of Japan's 57 million people lived in the maze of villages that dotted the islands from storm-ridden coasts to the rugged mountain regions.

"Brother Cowman, have the villages of Japan been given an opportunity to hear the gospel?" The question came from a missionary who spoke in halting Japanese during a language class Cowman was conducting. The query was like a flaming dart. It struck the soul of Charles Cowman and lodged there. He recalled the afternoon he had stood on a mountain overlooking a sea of villages and had been gripped by the word "Unreached, unreached." "Lord, use me to reach the villages of Japan," he had responded. Now the time had come to act. The class was turned into a prayer meeting.

At ten o'clock that night Cowman went to his room. Midnight came and his wife urged him to retire, but he was too troubled for sleep. "The burden of my heart is too great," he said. "I wish to be alone."

At dawn Charles Cowman greeted his wife with a cheery "Good morning," informing her that during the night God had shown him how to reach every creature in Japan with the gospel. Then he called together his fellow missionaries to unburden his soul.

"We have skirted only the borders of Japan," he began. "Eighty percent of the people have never heard one word of the gospel and this condition exists after sixty years of missionary effort."

Then he continued: "We are going to place the Word of God in every home in the Japanese empire. God has given me a plan."

In his businesslike manner he had jotted down the following statistics which he presented to the missionaries:

Population of Japan	57,000,000
Number of homes	10,320,000
Cost of Scriptures and expense of workers	$100,000

Then Cowman outlined the plan God had shown him:

Young volunteers from the United States would be called to work with teams of ten national workers. Together they would cover Japan by foot, taking the Word of Life to every home throughout the provinces. "It should take about six months to cover a province," Cowman estimated.

Once Cowman had set his mind to the gigantic undertaking, nothing could deter him. He issued a plea for young men—crusaders who would work with teams of Japanese evangelists. One by one they responded.

The fact that there was only $5.00 in the mission treasury did not dampen Cowman's enthusiasm. When asked where the money was to come from, he simply pointed to his proposed source of supply: Mark 11:23, "Have faith in God."

The Great Village Campaign, as it became known, was an unprecedented epoch in the history of modern missions. Some called the attempt "foolhardy"; others ridiculed it as being visionary and impractical. Nevertheless, God was dramatically in it.

Tokyo was the first target of the crusade teams. After the city was covered, the twelve crusaders with their team of nationals began their strenuous cross-country trek. With bags of gospels slung over their shoulders, they walked from home to home, sleeping at night in crowded Japanese inns. At the end of four months the first province had been covered. Millions had heard of Jesus Christ for the first time; nine hundred had sought Him as Saviour.

The cost of supporting twelve teams of workers and purchasing millions of Scripture portions put the faith of Charles Cowman to a new test. He welcomed the opportunity to prove again what he had always maintained: "It is not a question of supply and demand, but of the Supplier."

When at one point in the campaign he received word that there were "no funds on hand," his plan of action was simple. He immediately dispatched telegrams to the twelve team leaders calling for a "Sabbath day of prayer." While the workers retired to Japanese inns to pray, Cowman himself went to his knees; there he spent the entire night. They did not have long to wait. By Monday morning a messenger was at the door, telegram in hand. It read: "Dr. T. has sent $8,000 for the Village Campaign."

On another occasion a judge in the South was awakened with a burden for the work of Cowman and Kilbourne. He could not escape the impression that God would have him do something. Unable to return to sleep, he rose and mailed a check for $3,000 to cover the expense of reaching a province with the gospel. When reports of the campaign reached the judge, he promptly mailed another $2,000. The progress of the teams was charted on a large map of Japan, and with each fresh victory Charles praised God for the realization of a cherished dream.

Charles Cowman's success as a missionary "General" was rooted in an intimate relationship with his Lord which gave to his leadership an authority that commanded respect. His life and ministry were characterized by a consistency that drew this beautiful, if ungrammatical, tribute from a national co-worker:

"Brother Cowman always alike," testified the Japanese brother, "all over alike, never change, no fall down, no wobble, all the same every year. For this I like very much. Five year, not matter, ten year no matter, twenty-five year no matter. Christianity never change for him. I see him every day always smile, always work, always try to get souls. Praise the Lord.''

He was a prodigious man of prayer, and Lettie described his faith as "simple, almost childlike." He obtained it by constant converse with God in reading of His Word, a habit which he began when he first met the Lord. Whenever a subject for controversy came up, he would invariably say, "Let us go to the Word of God for the answer." It gave him direction in all the affairs of the mission as well as those of his own life. The Bible was to him complete, authoritative, final. No book in the Bible was read more than Acts of the Apostles and it was his belief that the gospel is just as effective now as in the Apostolic days.

Charles Cowman kept up a voluminous correspondence with friends and fellow missionaries. His letters, a treasure in themselves, provide rich insights into the spirit of the man. These letters are full of tender sympathy. "Many a defeated soul took shelter in his heart," his wife said. But when the situation demanded it, he could do the most difficult task of all; he could rebuke a friend without jeopardizing a personal friendship.

To a discouraged missionary he wrote, "We cannot minister to our fellowmen if we are not constantly ministered to by Jesus himself. How about your private prayer life? And are you attentive at testimony meetings?

When a missionary was tempted to leave his flock, Cowman asked him, "Forgive me if I write plainly right out of my heart. You have met a life crisis to be sure, but should such a man as you, redeemed, sanctified, called of God to be an ambassador, flee from your corner of the field just because the battle waxed hot?"

And to one who complained of spiritual leanness, he addressed these words: "You tell me that your experience has cooled off. Forgive me, Brother, but I have known it for months...I fear that you have been mixing up in too many things, lawful in themselves, but not expedient...there are many things in your life that are only waste; these ought to be cut off. 'Narrow' shall you be called? Yes, doubtless, but I would make a clean sweep of everything and be content to be termed 'narrow-minded.' ''

Writing to a fellow missionary who was dealing with an erring brother he cautioned, "Hard missionaries are not of much use; they are not like the Master. He is never hard. It is better to be trusting, gentle, and sympathizing, even if often taken in, than to be sharp and hard. . .let it not be said of us that we are holy but hard.''

By 1918 the Great Village Campaign in Japan was completed, and evangelistic teams were moving across Korea, where the OMS had established a Bible training center in a similar effort. But now the strenuous pace was beginning to tell on Charles Cowman. The boundless energy with which he had driven himself began to ebb away. The house of flesh was no longer able to keep pace with the seething passion of his soul.

''I cannot rest while they die,'' Charles Cowman once told a colleague. It was this relentless purpose that so impressed those who knew him best.

The beloved author, Oswald Chambers, said, ''The thing that strikes you about Charles Cowman is his absolutely reckless, careless, defiant abandonment to Jesus Christ.''

One missionary recalled that ''Whenever the evangelization of the Orient was mentioned his soul took fire and you felt he would die a martyr through his own fervidness. . .he belonged to the class of early martyrs whose passionate love for souls made an early holocaust of the physical man.'' Said another, ''He was on fire for souls. I do not know that he ever took a vacation from the time he went to the mission field until his fatal breakdown.''

Cowman's days in Japan were rapidly drawing to a close. On August 15, 1917, he made the following entry in his diary: ''Experienced a strange pain in my heart in the night, but prayed and it left me. I can see no place to stop in this work.''

Within a year, however, he found it impossible to continue. ''Worn out,'' was the doctor's diagnosis. Only an immediate change of climate and a prolonged rest would save his life, the physician warned.

Early one morning that fall, Charles Cowman, with his wife, Lettie, boarded the steamer that was to take him forever from his beloved island home. A group of workers and students was there, and Mrs. Cowman recalled they felt a ''strange presentiment'' that their next meeting would be in the presence of the King; but Charles bade them farewell with the same old cheery smile and assured them that he would be well and back at his post again.

On the boat, he turned to his wife. ''I love them so dearly,'' he wept. "How utterly vain to express the emotion of my soul. No, never can any finite being know, never."

In California, Charles Cowman recovered a measure of health, and with strength came an irresistible urge to communicate the burden of the Orient to Christians in America. He set out. For six months he mounted platforms from California to Michigan, telling the miracle story of the Village Campaign.

Everywhere he went he carried a great map of Japan and Korea. Standing beside it he would point to the areas marked in red—indicating the provinces covered by the crusade teams. Often he would break down and weep as he recalled the struggles and triumphs.

But the candle of life was burning low. That summer while on a train nearing Owosso, Michigan, he was stricken with a severe heart attack and was unable to proceed. "You must stop your public work at once," the doctor insisted. "Return to California and rest. Frankly," he added, "your work is at an end."

His public ministry over, Charles Cowman's faith was to be put to the ultimate test; for six torturous years God would prove him in the crucible of suffering. In the prison of his room and under the wearing shackles of pain and weakness, Charles Cowman was to understand the mysterious dealing of the One he had so often recommended to others.

From all over the world came letters with the inevitable query—a question that must often have found an echo in the soul of the dying missionary: "Why, why should God's worker be cut down so suddenly? Why, when the work so needed him?"

Charles Cowman was not to know the full answer to that question —not during his earthly life. But the millions who have been blessed through the readings of Lettie Cowman's *Streams in the Desert* can perhaps discern something of God's ways. Through those six long years of agony, Lettie, the valiant wife and nurse, made her collection—a treasury of poems and readings that was destined to minister to the fainting hearts of millions of other sufferers.

But all this Charles Cowman could not see; without sight he demonstrated an unshakable faith that is fixed upon a God who is love itself and cannot deny Himself.

"Charles Cowman," wrote his wife, "was great as a businessman;

he was great before audiences; he was great on the mission field; but he was greatest when shut away alone with God in the loneliness of the desert.''

Once he turned to his companion to whisper, ''God gave me a song in the night and I have found sweet music even in the solitudes of a sick room.''

The sick room became a sanctuary of prayer. On the wall before the invalid hung a large map of the world and across the fields of the Orient Cowman had written, ''Without God and without hope 450,000,000 eternity-bound souls for whom I am responsible.'' For these he prayed with the kind of burden that reflected a genuine sense of personal accountability. Turning to a visitor he once remarked, ''What must the Master think of us as He looks down upon that map that represents the millions of heathendom? What does He think of me?''

The unrelieved pain did not dim his missionary vision. His wife found him one evening in his study with his face buried in his hands, quietly weeping. On his desk was a map of the Orient wet with tears. He handed her the following poem:

> Let me go back. I am homesick
> For the land of my love and toil
> Though I thrill at the sight of my native hills
> The touch of my native soil
> Thank God for the dear home-country
> Unconquered free and grand!
> But the far-off shores of Japan for me
> Are the shores of my promised land.

In the fifth year of his illness, Cowman wrote, ''The best hours of my illness have been when the fierce fires of suffering are kindling and scorching all around me. How soothing in the midst of suffering to feel hour after hour the soul-cleansing blood of the Lamb.'' And with suffering came the growing conviction that ''This valley has been planned for me, provided for me and is the very best place, for the Lord is with me even here and I can stake my all upon God's faithfulness...In His moment He will say, 'It is enough.' ''

That moment came a year later on September 23, 1924. But before his passing, Charles Cowman addressed final words to his wife and friends.

To his friend and beloved colleague, E. A. Kilbourne, who had just returned from Japan, he said, "What comrades we have been throughout the years! Our hearts have been knit together; no, knit is not the word. Our hearts were 'burned' together...I have no regret that my life is slipping away because of what I have done for my heathen brothers. I am glad, oh so glad."

To his wife he made this tender plea: "Don't let the song go out of your life, my love; for your sake, for others' sake. And maybe I, too, shall hear and be glad."

The last words he addressed to his fellow missionaries were these: "I am so convinced that the work is God's that nothing from without can by any means harm it, but you must stay very close together and at the foot of the Cross where there is none of self but all of Christ. You can harm it if you allow disunity among yourselves, looking after your own personal interests and failing to be true to the vision God has given us...Disunity cannot live in an atmosphere of love."

When word of Charles Cowman's death reached Japan, the church felt deeply the loss of their leader and friend. "We have lost our kind, loving shepherd and the flock is bleating," wrote one national Christian who seemed to speak for the entire church.

Though their leader was gone, the flock was not left without shepherds—well-trained and Spirit-led. It was as Cowman had planned it. He had done his work wisely and well.

2

Juji Nakada

The burly fisherman glanced down the narrow street, noting the group of townspeople gathering in the small market place. A stocky youth, hardly five feet tall, was addressing them excitedly.

"Who's that fellow over there?" the fisherman growled, thrusting his chin in the direction of the crowd.

"Some fanatic," his companion replied. "A Christian preacher. They call him Nakada."

The big man smiled. "So that's Nakada. I think we can teach that boy to talk about the sins of the people of Chishima!"

His comrade caught the mischief in his eye and winked back approval. The two men, joined by a handful of bystanders, moved cautiously toward the market place.

Nakada saw the man coming—elbowing his way toward him through the crowd. He braced himself for what he had long known would come sooner or later, but went on preaching.

With the fisherman's first lunge, Nakada went into action. Diverting the attach with a subtle shift of his weight, he executed a simple judo maneuver with the casual artistry of an expert. An instant later his attacker was sprawling ignominiously on the street. The onlookers observed the fisherman's plight with a roar of delight.

The young preacher's name was Juji Nakada. The name would one day be known in every Christian household in Japan. For his fearless preaching and dynamic leadership, thousands would acknowledge a debt of gratitude.

Those who heard Juji Nakada preach often referred to him as "The Dwight L. Moody of Japan." Many insist that next to Gumpei Yamamuro of the Salvation Army, Nakada was the greatest evangelistic preacher Japan has ever known.

And in the unfolding miracle of The Oriental Missionary Society, this intense little man with burning eyes had been chosen of God to play a key role. With Charles Cowman and E. A. Kilbourne, he would be used to lay the foundation upon which a great church and a far-flung missionary organization would rise.

Juji Nakada was born in 1870 in Hirosake, Japan. His father, a *Samurai* (feudal lord) was described as "a hot-tempered, quarrelsome drunkard who was never able to advance in rank." He died leaving his wife with three sons, the youngest of whom was Juji. To support her family, Mrs. Nakada took in sewing and carried vegetables into town where she sold them for a small income. These trips brought her in contact with a Christian pastor, Yoichi Honda, who befriended the impoverished family.

The unusual ministry of Juji Nakada is, in part, a tribute to his life-long friend and mentor, Yoichi Honda. Here was a pastor of remarkable vision coupled with a practical faith. His church in Hirosake produced no fewer than seventy ministers, among them Nakada and his brother. Honda later became an influential Christian educator, and as a church leader he brought about the union of three large Methodist bodies into a single, powerful denomination of which he became bishop. Such was the instrument God used to shape the early life of Juji Nakada.

Through the ministry of Rev. Honda, Nakada's two older brothers were converted. The oldest became a Methodist minister; the second died shortly after his conversion. Young Juji, however, was a mischievous rascal and a great trial to his mother. Neighbors remembered that he delighted in dousing passers-by with dirty dish water. Nevertheless, Honda managed to convince the ardent Buddhist mother that a Christian Sunday school would solve her youngest son's behavior problem. During his teens, Juji finally yielded to the pressure of God's Spirit and opened his heart to Christ. Now he begged his mother to come to church. Neighbors urged her to avoid the pernicious Christian doctrine. But, "Certainly," she reasoned, "the religion that has done so much for my sons can do me no harm." The next Sunday she accompanied Juji to church and was soundly converted—the first of thousands that Juji Nakada would lead to the Saviour.

Although Juji Nakada was now certain of his faith in Christ, he found himself caught in a new conflict. The checkered pattern of events that crowd the following years reveal a soul torn between the tumultuous ambitions of youth and a full and final surrender to the mastery of Jesus Christ. It was a contest that would more than once see the young life driven to the brink of disobedience and spiritual disaster.

While still in his early teens, Juji left home to assist his brother, then a pastor in the town of Amori. But Juji did not stay long. By the time he was fifteen he had decided to pursue the life of a seaman. Leaving Amori, he set out for the port city of Hakadoti, where he signed up as a sailor aboard an outbound vessel. But Juji Nakada's career as a seaman was short lived. It took one experience with the savage ferocity of a Pacific typhoon and an acute case of seasickness to convince him of the advantages of a landsman's lot.

Juji was eighteen when his friend, Rev. Honda, was made president of a large Methodist school in Tokyo known as "Aoyama Gakuin" University. Although Nakada had finished no more than eight years of schooling at this time, at Honda's urging he applied to the university and was admitted. He first elected to study in the field of English literature; a short time later, however, he sensed God calling him into the ministry and changed to a theological course.

Student days for the restless lad were colorful and strenuous. His regular weekend activities were feats that reveal the remarkable energies with which he was endowed. After finishing classes Saturday afternoons, he would hike thirty miles through the night to the town of Kumagaya where his brother was then pastoring. Arriving in time to teach Sunday school, he would thereafter participate in the morning worship service. In the afternoons, he conducted street meetings and assisted his brother in visitation. Only after the long evening service did he begin the return trip, walking again all night in order to make the Monday morning lecture at the university. On these jaunts he somehow found time to pursue his hobby of archeology, stopping along the road to unearth anything that aroused his curiosity.

The lure of adventure often enticed Nakada and his companions up the steep slopes of majestic Mount Fuji. On one unforgettable afternoon, he and a friend were overtaken by a sudden tropical storm. Rain whipped their bodies with savage force. Nakada recalled that "the gale became so violent it blew my coat off. It was almost impossible to stand against it." Thrusting a strong arm around his younger companion, Juji started a tortuous descent, crawling along until they managed to reach the refuge of a cave. "How easily we could both have been killed," Nakada later said.

Death, once cheated, seemed determined to have satisfaction. A short time later, while swimming in the ocean, Nakada was seized in the grip of a powerful undertow. Helpless in the treacherous current, he found himself being swept out to sea. At last, too exhausted to swim, he gave a final desperate cry, "Oh, God, help me. Help me!" The cry attracted the attention of a fisherman in the nearby waters who quickly plunged in after the drowning student and hauled him aboard his small craft.

These brushes with death were followed by a weird sequel that left Juji Nakada deeply grieved, but shocked into a new sense of destiny. Two of his fellow students, both in ministerial training, were tragically killed. The first died while climbing a mountain. The other was drowned.

Now, it seemed that the enemy resorted to more subtle tactics in an effort to divert Nakada from God's chosen course for his life. Juji Nakada had fallen in love. He had given his heart with characteristic abandon to the lovely daughter of a wealthy noble—a gentleman who had no son of his own. When it appeared that Nakada was intent on marriage, the man appealed to him with a tempting proposition: "I want you to be my son," he assured Juji warmly. "You may have my daughter, wealth, and an influential career. All I ask is that you give up the ministry, enter Tokyo University, and prepare for diplomatic service."

The lush offer presented Juji Nakada with an agonizing decision. What would he do? He was certain of his love for God and his call to the ministry. He was also convinced of his love for the girl.

"Give me time to think it over," he pleaded.

Nakada and the girl arranged to meet at a future date. By then, he assured her, he would be prepared to announce his decision. Perhaps

Nakada had a premonition of what was to follow. The place he chose to meet the girl was an unusual one—a graveyard!

On the appointed night, Nakada found his sweetheart waiting for him and eager for his decision.

"I love God," he began simply. "I cannot consider giving up the ministry. He has called me to preach. But, I also love you and I am unwilling to let you go. I cannot make the decision," he concluded, "you must make the choice."

This unexpected turn of events left the girl bewildered. She proceeded to faint on the spot.

Juji Nakada was desperate for her answer when they met again. This time she had her reply ready. "You must forget me," she announced abruptly. "I cannot marry a preacher. However, you have my younger sister, instead. She can become a preacher's wife, but not I."

The prospect of the future without the one he loved plunged Nakada into a mood of despair. Even the sympathy his closest friends offered seemed poor comfort. And when he learned of the girl's marriage to a Tokyo University graduate, life seemed to be robbed of purpose.

"I can't continue," he confessed to President Honda. "I've decided to quit school and return to the sea."

But the man to whom Nakada already owed so much again proved an invaluable friend, offering the heartbroken student the steadying counsel that the hour required.

Juji Nakada had no sooner weathered this crisis than he found himself involved in an unhappy imbroglio that resulted in his expulsion from school. The problem stemmed from Juji's aversion to certain courses in Biblical criticism. This so-called "higher criticism," originating in Germany, had invaded theological schools in both the United States and Japan, casting doubt upon the authority and inspiration of the Scriptures. Nakada abhorred these classes and all his life he remained a vigorous opponent of liberalism. He began devoting more and more time to two favorite activities, judo and oratory. Meanwhile, he was conspicuously absent from classes in Biblical criticism. This sort of conduct invoked the wrath of his teachers (notably several missionaries), who demanded the young rebel be dismissed from school.

President Honda, unable to prevent the inevitable, decided on a shrewd, if unusual, course of action.

"I have no choice but to dismiss you from school," he told Nakada, "but you can still be a preacher. We need someone to do pioneer evangelism on Chishima. There are only two Christians on the islands. Are you interested?

"Chishima," Nakada echoed, "that's the very place I've always wanted to go." (Chishima is the name for the rugged Kuril Islands, which extend in a far-flung arc between the northern coast of Japan and Russia.) To the adventuresome youth, Chishima spelled excitement, the rigorous life he found so appealing. In a short time Juji Nakada, the rebel expellee, was appointed by the Methodist Church to what was, without a doubt, the most rugged parish in all Japan, the Kuril Islands.

In Chishima, Nakada soon adapted to the strenuous life for which he was already so well prepared. His prowess in judo won him the respect of the rough fishermen who were soon vying with one another for the honor of serving as his bodyguards during street meetings. For the young people, Juji held classes in judo and archery, winning their admiration and a chance to preach Christ to them—an opportunity he never missed.

Evangelistic trips to isolated fishing villages took him across desolate stretches of wasteland and over remote mountain ranges. "Climbing up the icy mountains," he remembered, "was very laborious, but sliding down on the other side was sheer pleasure." Night often found him on some forsaken slope, far from home with only a dog and rifle as protection against marauding bears. Experiences that would have disheartened ordinary men were welcomed as a hearty challenge by the young evangelist.

Like the Methodist circuit riders, Nakada carried books wherever he went, often studying as he traveled. A fisherman named Giichi Ishida remembered the day Nakada gave him a few volumes in exchange for salmon skin shoes. These shoes, Ishida explained, were unusually valuable commodities; they could be worn as waterproof footwear or roasted and eaten if the occasion demanded. "Nakada impressed me with his tremendous energy," said Ishida. "He would often stop by and help me. How the man could work!" Today, Giichi Ishida is a preacher of the gospel in Brazil. In a letter to Nakada's son, he revealed, "It was your father's life and zeal that inspired me to consecrate myself to God for the ministry."

Among the fishermen Juji won for himself both friendship and a reputation for raw courage. One evening he was informed that two of the townsmen were involved in a fight. Rushing out, he found the fishermen in a vicious brawl. The bigger fellow was slashing at his opponent with a small sword. Without hesitation, Nakada plunged into the melee, disarming and subduing the attacker. He emerged from the struggle unscathed but, he lamented with typical good humor, "My only good kimono was cut to shreds in the fray."

In 1894, after opening his Chishima work, Nakada returned to Tokyo for his ordination. At the same time, he also took a bride, Katsuko Odote, an outstanding Christian and the daughter of a feudal lord. They had met at a women's high school at Hakadote where she taught and where Juji had for a time worked as janitor. The match was a good one. Katsuko proved an excellent mother and a faithful wife until her early death at the age of 42.

Juji had taken Katsuko back with him to Chishima. Daily life, like the topography of the islands, was rough and bleak. But the new bride was a genuine helpmeet and a woman of real character; she suffered without complaint the burden of poor health and the loss of their first child, a baby girl who died in infancy.

Katsuko's failing health, however, eventually made it necessary for the Nakadas to return to the main island of Hokkaido where Juji took a pastorate. There a son, Ugo, was born to them, a life destined to make a rich contribution in the field of church music in Japan.

By the time Juji Nakada was 26, he was in his fourth pastorate. Apparently successful, he nevertheless found himself increasingly dissatisfied with his ministry. He had heard of the great soul winner, D. L. Moody, and a question gnawed at his consciousness, "What was Moody's secret?"

The question festered in his mind until he became strangely restless. Even his wife noticed it.

"What is it that's troubling you?" she asked one day. "For so long now, you've hardly said a word."

"I must go to America," Nakada replied.

"But why?"

"To be filled with the Holy Spirit. If there is one who can help me, his name is Mr. Moody. The only problem," he ended slowly, "I have no money."

Unknown to Nakada, his wife had received a generous sum of money from her father at the time of their marriage. This she had hidden away for an unseen emergency.

"I have the money," she told her husband, explaining about the gift. "But," she continued, "what if you fail to get this experience you seek? What will you do then?"

"Without the power of the Holy Spirit in my life," Nakada answered with conviction, "I cannot continue in the ministry. So if I fail, I will then study to become a dentist." But Juji Nakada was not to be denied. Immediately he made plans to go to the United States. In his absence, his wife resumed teaching to support herself and their small son.

Juji Nakada arrived at Moody Bible Institute in 1897, two years before the death of D. L. Moody. "The first question asked me by one of the professors," he wrote, "was, 'Have you been baptized with the Holy Ghost?' I knew I had not and was seeking a better experience. He told me that the baptism of the Holy Ghost empowered us for service; but what I need even more than power is cleansing. There is something wrong in my nature, but I don't know the cause of the trouble."

His search for the "better experience" took him to the nearby Grace Methodist Church and a historic meeting with the young telegrapher, Charles Cowman. That day began a rich friendship out of which grew the beginnings of The Oriental Missionary Society in Japan. And more than any other individual, Juji Nakada was used of God to fire the soul of Charles Cowman for the Orient. Only eternity will reveal the consequences of the divinely-ordained meeting.

Cowman invited the Japanese student to the Bible class where he assured him the baptism of the Holy Spirit would be discussed in the light of the Scriptures.

"There it was that I discovered my problem," testified Nakada. "What I really needed was a complete cleansing—heart holiness."

He began a diligent study of the doctrine of heart purity, devouring as many books as he could find on the subject. "I was especially helped," he said, "by reading the works of B. Carradine, A. M. Hills, and John Wesley, until light came and I understood the doctrine plainly.''

It happened on November 21, 1897—the event that would transform the life and ministry of Juji Nakada, making of the frustrated Methodist preacher an instrument of power through which God would touch multitudes of Orientals for Christ.

The chapel speaker at the Moody Institute that day was an Indian evangelist, V. A. David, and the service was followed by testimonies from the students. While others witnessed, Nakada admitted to himself that he was miserable. ''Why have I no joy?'' he asked. ''Why can I not sing?'' Nevertheless, he resolutely stood to his feet. ''I praise God,'' he said, ''for putting the hunger and thirst for righteousness in my soul. God will surely meet my need just as He promised.''

With that, Juji Nakada hurried to his room where he threw himself on the floor praying and weeping. Eleven years later he testified, ''The blessing came that day; my bedroom was the place and my bed the altar. God sanctified my soul.'' There followed a swift realization that he had been entirely cleansed. Then, ''unspeakable peace.'' Late that night his neighbors complained that the fellow from Japan was keeping them awake with his songs and shouts of joy.

Nakada had previously planned to remain in the United States for graduate study following the completion of his year at Moody. But now the urge to return to Japan seized him. He had found what he had come to America to get. ''My plans were entirely changed when I got the best thing in the world,'' he said. ''I had received the Holy Ghost.''

At the end of the school year, Nakada prepared to return to Japan. He was tempted to pay expenses by lecturing on Japan, as other Japanese students were doing. But this, he decided, would be less than ''trusting fully in God.'' Instead, he started on an evangelistic tour, preaching wherever he found churches open to him. ''I could not speak English well,'' he admitted, ''but the Lord wonderfully blessed me. Souls were saved and sanctified.''

Arriving in New York, he took stock of his resources. He had no money left, only his faith in God. ''How to get across the ocean was my problem,'' he confessed. ''It was too far to swim. I had no money to pay my passage. So I decided to become a cowhand.''

He managed to get a job tending stock on a reeking cattle boat bound for London. The *Michigan* was the vessel's name. Her cargo:

100 horses and 500 head of cattle.

Nakada described his fellow cowhands as "wicked men, tramps, and rascals. I never met such an ungodly crowd in my life." And to make matters worse, Nakada was a hopeless sailor. "I was sick nearly all the time," he wrote.

Now the self-sufficient young preacher whose judo prowess had awed the rough fishermen of Chishima was being subjected to the supreme test, humiliation. Physical hardship he was well acquainted with, but sheer humiliation was a new experience. Juji Nakada was tasting the "fellowship of His sufferings." He would be a better man for it.

Aboard the *Michigan,* he found himself an object of contempt and the butt of crude jokes. "Whenever I tried to rest," he recorded, "the boss would come around and kick me. Then the cowboys would kick me. And the horses and cows kicked me, too. The other cowboys didn't work much and, as I was the only Oriental on board, they made me do most of the work."

At mealtime, the stronger men would grab a huge share of the food, leaving Nakada and the weaker ones to scramble over the remains and often do without.

One day a cowhand, while snooping through Nakada's trunk, found a letter addressed to "Rev. Juji Nakada."

"A preacher!" he scoffed, "don't tell me you're a minister."

"Yes, I am a minister," replied Juji, bracing himself.

"What kind of a minister are you."

"A Christian minister."

"Hey," the cowhand shouted to his buddies, "we have a reverend in our midst. Let's have him preach us a sermon."

The next Sunday, Nakada mounted a bale of hay to preach a gospel message. "I never saw such an audience in all my life," he said. "At every word I spoke, they would swear and laugh and mock in religious language. They did not have any respect for my preaching. I did not get any converts among them. But a backslidden engineer, whom I finally found, was kind to me and would get me meat to eat. It was the only salary I got for my preaching."

Nakada arrived in London a sorry sight. "I looked like a beggar," he said. "There was no time to clean myself on the boat, I had to work so long. I had slept with the cattle on the hay, so my clothing stunk and I smelt very bad.''

In desperation, he made his way to the home of a Christian gentleman whose address he had been given. His humbling was complete when a servant, thinking him a vagabond, turned him away at the door.

After some effort, however, Nakada managed to gain entrance to the home, where he was warmly welcomed, fed, clothed, and helped on his way. From England he proceeded to work his way to Japan as a cabin boy on another steamer. Aboard, he encountered an old hometown acquaintance. The man was Baron Chinda, then Japan's Vice-Minister of Foreign Affairs.

"What class are you traveling?" asked Chinda.

"No class," replied Nakada, "I'm working my way to Japan as a cabin boy."

"A cabin boy. How is it that a minister must work as a cabin boy?"

"I have no money."

"Well then," smiled Chinda, "you'll be my guest. I'll pay your way."

"Oh, no," protested Juji Nakada, "that's against my principles. I believe this is the way God wants me to travel."

Chinda was impressed. Throughout the voyage he delighted in showing the "cabin boy" special favors, leaving the other passengers confounded by such irregular conduct. During the stopover in Hong Kong, Nakada saw the city in tow of his influential friend. "I was treated like a government official," he said, "which was quite a change after the cattle boat experience."

It was a new Juji Nakada who rejoined his family in Japan and set out upon an independent ministry of evangelism. In place of the impulsive, oft-frustrated young preacher appeared a man of maturity, firm conviction, and unusual power. As an evangelist, he found a natural and satisfying outlet for his fervid temperament. But, more than this, his success can only be attributed to the work of the Holy Spirit in his life. Now he preached with a holy unction and compelling force that friends agreed had not been part of the old Juji Nakada.

God blessed. Notwithstanding his fearless, sometimes tactless, denouncements of worldliness, people came to hear "the man from Moody." Wherever he preached, they crowded their way into the narrow halls and churches. And at the invitation they made their way to the altar, often weeping under the weight of conviction.

Reports of these services were faithfully returned to Charles Cowman and the band of telegraphers who had taken it upon themselves to support Nakada in his new work. Then in 1901, in a surprising course of events, Charles Cowman was led of God to Japan. The two men, strikingly alike in mind and spirit, joined forces. They shared a common vision for a Bible school patterned after the Moody Institute both had attended in Chicago. Their mutual objective: to train Spirit-filled nationals who could effectively win their own people to the Master.

It was Nakada more than anyone else who convinced Cowman that the missionary's prime task was to train nationals and establish an indigenous church. "Charles Cowman recognized this fact," said his wife, "as he witnessed the effectiveness of Juji Nakada's preaching to his own people. The establishment of an aggressive and vigorous native church became the burden of his soul."

"Would that you might have been with us in our service last night," wrote Cowman shortly after the opening of their new work. "The altar was crowded with earnest seekers. Every seat in the hall was occupied and the window spaces were filled. Nakada was the preacher and he is a master of the crowd."

The first task that faced Nakada and Cowman was to locate their new Bible school and evangelistic center. Finding a suitable building with a reasonable rental and a landlord willing to lease it to Christians was no small task in Tokyo. Their search took them on a foot-wearying tramp through the city's vast complex of alleys and clotted thoroughfares.

At one point Cowman is reported to have turned to Nakada to inquire, "What is the name of this part of Tokyo."

"This is *Kanda,*" replied Nakada.

"What does that mean?"

"The character means god and field."

"Then we shall begin our work here," concluded Cowman, "in God's field."

A little farther, Cowman asked, "What is the name of this street?" Nakada glanced at the sign. "*Jimbo Cho*—Street of God's support." Both men seemed to feel that this must be the location God had chosen for their work. Before long they found a large building for rent and, more important, a landlord happy to lease it to Christians. They had no more than concluded the transaction when a man arrived in a ricksha intent on renting the building. "It was a case of perfectly timed guidance," Cowman wrote.

Charles Cowman and Juji Nakada were bold in their expectations. They were convinced that the message of Jesus Christ preached with conviction would work in the hearts of men anywhere—even in the Jimbo Cho section of Tokyo. Nor were they disappointed. Within the first month the hall was open, almost a hundred seekers walked down the narrow aisles to find Christ at the altar.

Six years later Cowman's co-worker, E. A. Kilbourne, reported: "Mission No. 1 has been in existence since the day the Bible school was opened, and there has been a meeting every night of the year, over 2,400 nights without a break. Hardly a night has passed but what souls have been at the altar."

On trips abroad, Nakada encountered converts from that first mission in every land he touched and in every province in the empire of Japan, including Korea and Formosa.

The large building in the Jimbo Cho district also housed the new Bible school. The institute was opened by Nakada and Cowman in 1901 with an enrollment of four students. Nakada decided the school should be promoted through *Hono O No Shita* (Tongues of Fire), a little magazine he had begun publishing several years earlier. *Hono O No Shita* sought to stimulate Christians' interest in such themes as heart purity, the filling of the Holy Spirit, the second coming of Christ, healing, and prayer. Though the circulation never was large, the little magazine exerted a surprising influence upon the churches of Japan. Through *Hono O No Shita,* scores of hungry-hearted young people learned of the unique Bible institute with its emphasis on practical training and the Spirit-filled life. Soon they were applying. They came from every province of Japan and from distant points—China, Formosa, Korea.

One day two strange looking gentlemen appeared at the Bible school in Tokyo. They wore ridiculous looking, stiff, wide-brimmed horsehair hats; long white gowns; white, bulky bloomer-type trousers tied at the ankles; and shoes with pointed, turned-up toes. Cowman and Kilbourne had never seen the like. Obviously, they were not Japanese and they spoke in a language that was unintelligible. Cowman and Kilbourne answered in Japanese, which the men could not understand. Finally they tried English, but again without success. There was a long pause. Then one gentleman's face lit up.

"Hallelujah," he shouted.

"Amen," Cowman and Kilbourne responded instinctively.

They had found a mutual language. Soon it was discovered that the men could write Chinese characters common to Korea, Japan, and China. Thus it was learned that their strange-looking visitors were from Korea. They had heard Juji Nakada preach in Korea and had come to the Japan Bible Institute "to learn more about the Bible and the Holy Spirit." Very soon they did two things: They learned Japanese and wrote back to Korea of the wonderful school they had found. As a result, three other Korean pastors arrived, seeking training for more effective ministry to their people.

Nakada demanded of the students a rigid discipline and daily participation in practical soul-winning efforts. The curriculum of the institute reflects his own energetic disposition and the Moody Institute emphasis on "field training."

In a brief account of a week at the Bible school, Mrs. Cowman recorded the exhausting schedule of activities:

"On Sunday," she wrote, "students are up at 5 a.m.—a bell summons the soldiers of the Cross to the battlefield. Already some have slipped away to keep their tryst with the 'chiefest among ten thousand.' "

The day was spent in a strenuous round of activities that took students to cottage meetings, open-air services, and Sunday schools. One was held "under a large tree with spreading branches in a slum neighborhood where more than 100 children attend."

"That evening," Mrs. Cowman continued, "the fronts of the stores and shops were wide open and at our street meetings on three different corners we had crowds of several hundred. It was a night of victory and the Lord set His seal to the messages. A good-sized throng followed into the mission where everything was in readiness for the evening battle. Every available seat was filled and strips of matting spread in the front were soon filled. How the hall rang with songs of the power of redeeming grace.

"Conviction was plainly written upon many a face and before preaching began, 17 expressed a desire to be saved. Brother Nakada brought a message fresh from the throne, and the altar was filled two rows deep with seekers.''

Weekday mornings in the school were given to study, primarily Bible study. Classes took the character of devotional fellowships made exciting by the union of like minds, bound by a common Lord, a common passion. The spirit of these sessions is caught in Mrs. Cowman's diary: "Eight a.m. Tuesday—the students all gather for their classes. We study this morning 'The Coming of our Lord,' a subject spoken of 320 times in the New Testament . . . it is a blessed hour and we see even more clearly that 'His coming draweth nigh.' ''

Afternoons found the students again out in the field in an exhausting round of Christian activities. Believers were followed up with house calls. Bands of students were dispatched to outlying areas with bags of gospel tracts in distribution campaigns. Others held meetings in hospitals, orphanages, or under the sky in Ueno park or in the great temple courtyards.

Saturday evenings, however, provided the highlight of the week. "This is the time when all meet to wait on God in prayer and fasting," wrote Mrs. Cowman. "O what precious times we have in these half nights of prayer.''

Such was the atmosphere in which Nakada's Bible institute took root and flourished. It was a scene of constant activity. The hugeness of Cowman and Nakada's faith was contagious. Students were inspired to demand great things from God; to expect them. They seemed endued with the spirit of the first century Christians who, sensing the urgency of the times and realizing that they were ridiculously outnumbered, drew recklessly upon the power of the Holy Spirit.

The growing institute with its emphasis upon Spirit-filled national leadership met a large need in a day when the churches of Japan were infected with compromise engendered by liberal theology. Moreover, the formula of Nakada and Cowman was strikingly successful in producing capable national leaders. A year before Cowman's death, a prominent missionary stated, "The Oriental Missionary Society is better equipped with native leaders than any other mission in the Orient." At that time, no less than one thousand national preachers had been trained. Other denominations gave tacit recognition to the school by eagerly drawing upon the national leadership it was producing. Missionary statesman Paget Wilkes once remarked to an OMS missionary, "The greatest contribution your school has made has been outside your own church. Your graduates are filling key roles of leadership in every major evangelical denomination in Japan."

When the swelling student body outgrew the quarters at Jimbo Cho, Nakada joined with Cowman and Kilbourne in what was an unprecedented step of faith for the still-infant mission. With empty purses but unshakable confidence in God, they arranged for the purchase of a large property in the Shinjuku area of Tokyo, then on the outskirts of the city. The new location served as a campus for the Bible school and headquarters for the rapidly expanding church. This compound was the setting for veritable times of Pentecost when thousands of delegates from churches throughout Japan convened for the annual conference. Nakada was often the main speaker and the whole program was, for the most part, independent of the foreign missionary. "The campus seemed permeated with the presence of God," recalled one missionary who was present at those conventions.

From the Tokyo Bible Institute, graduates went out as pastors. Small congregations grew into flourishing mother churches, giving birth to scores of new congregations. In 1917, the Japan Holiness Church was organized (not to be confused with recent "holiness" movements characterized by an emphasis on speaking in tongues). Juji Nakada was elected the first bishop of the church, a position he held until his death in 1939. The growth of the church was spurred by two dramatic movements of the Holy Spirit that swept across the entire denomination. In both revivals, Juji Nakada was the instrument used of God to spread the fire.

By 1930 the Japan Holiness Church, under Nakada's leadership, had mushroomed to 403 churches with 400 additional preaching points and a total membership of 12,000. In 1930 alone, more than 4,000 believers were baptized, with another 3,400 in 1931. More impressive, by 1931 the church was entirely self-supporting and financially independent of The Oriental Missionary Society.

Ten years earlier, Nakada began a series of missionary and evangelistic tours. These missions took him four times to the United States and frequently to countries in the Far East. Moreover, the entire church had caught the missionary vision and at Nakada's urging had launched its own missionary movement. Missionaries from the Japan Holiness Church were sent to 12 foreign fields, among them Korea,

Manchuria, China, Formosa, and Okinawa.

As bishop, Nakada was an aggressive leader, always intensely evangelistic. It is not surprising that he was sometimes charged with being domineering, even dictatorial. But by the great majority of Christians, both laymen and clergy, he was held in respect that approached awe.

His genius as a leader is illustrated by a unique epoch in the history of the Japan Holiness Church. Nakada designated a certain day as "Each One Win One Day." The objective, he explained, was that on the appointed day, each member of the church was to make a concerted effort to win at least one soul to Christ. The people eagerly accepted the Bishop's challenge. Within the appointed 24-hour period, over 500 souls were won to Christ, many of them coming into the church.

From his own experience, Juji Nakada understood that the great secret of success in the life of both the individual Christian and the church is the baptism of the Holy Spirit. He accorded this doctrine the place of prominence that he was convinced God intended it to have. Sunday afternoons were given to the promotion of "scriptural holiness." During these services, the Spirit-filled life was preached with enthusiasm, and Christians were urged to enter into the second crisis experience. Such meetings were unprecedented in the Japanese church. And from all denominations and assorted classes, came the hungry-hearted school teachers, ministers, Bible women, even a viscountess. Through the viscountess, a ministry was begun among the royalty of Japan.

Nakada's success as administrator, evangelist, and church leader must be partially attributed to his ability to attract key men to his cause. These were frequently men with gifts that supplemented his own. Such was his early co-worker, the revered patriarch of the church, T. Sasao. A tall man, quiet by nature, Sasao understood the power of prayer. They first met at a large convention at which Nakada was the guest speaker. Nakada noticed a tall man enter the service. "Aren't you Mr. Sasao?" he called out. "Please come and help these seekers. We can meet afterwards."

One day in 1901, Sasao appeared at Nakada's newly opened Bible institute. "God said, 'Go,' so I came," he stated simply.

"But we have no money to support you," said Nakada.

"That makes no difference to me," returned Sasao, "I will trust God by faith."

Thus, T. Sasao joined forces with Cowman and Nakada. He became principal of the Bible school, making a rich contribution especially as a Bible scholar and author of numerous well-loved hymns.

From Moody, Nakada had learned how effective music could be as a vehicle of evangelism. During his messages, he often broke into song in his clear tenor voice. With Mr. Mitani, one of Barclay Buxton's workers, Nakada published the first book of gospel hymns ever made available in Japan.

But of all Juji Nakada's gifts, he will be best remembered for his rare ability to preach the gospel with unction and power. In the pulpit he was a man with few peers.

"In my estimation, Juji Nakada was a prince of preachers," says a missionary who knew him well. "The tone of his voice was of a commanding nature. He was apt in the use of illustrations and homiletical in his preaching."

"Juji Nakada was the most effective speaker I have ever heard," said university professor Dr. Zenta Watanabe, who was converted under Nakada's ministry. "He was a preacher with unusual persuasive powers."

His ability to carry his audience with him by his powers of descriptions recalls the preaching of George Whitefield. Once, while preaching on sin, Nakada compared the state of the lost to that of a drowning man caught in a tempest. "Conviction was mightily upon the audience," remembers one witness. "The people gripped the backs of the benches and when Nakada gestured as if throwing a lifeline to the drowning, several in the audience jumped up, grabbing for the imaginary rope and crying for help."

Another eyewitness tells of an Easter convention at which Nakada addressed over four thousand people. He reminded the audience that the newspapers of the land were full of the news of quarreling Buddhist sects of Japan who were claiming the right to receive and enshrine a piece of bone from the little finger of Buddha, which had been sent to the emperor by the king of Siam. Then with both hands raised towards heaven and the ring of Easter joy in his voice, Nakada cried, "Praise God! There are no bones of our Lord Jesus Christ remaining for people to quarrel and quibble about, for He is risen!"

The whole crowd was electrified. As one man, they rose to their feet with hands uplifted and shouted, "Hallelujah, hallelujah, He is risen!"

Nakada's messages were usually an hour in length. But Cowman wrote of a time when "Nakada preached for an hour and a half, and yet people lingered as if they did not wish to leave."

His resonant voice conveyed a warmth and compassion which some compared to D. L. Moody. And like Moody, he seasoned his messages with homey illustrations and an occasional trace of humor. He is still remembered for his pithy, insightful sayings. One of his favorites: "Your faith may be like iron, but if it is rusted, it is useless." Or, "A believer without a testimony is like a bicycle without a bell."

In addition to teaching, preaching, writing, administering, and traveling, Nakada found time for a variety of other activities. An opportunist for Christ, he was at the front lines during the Russo-Japanese War, taking the Word of Life to the troops. The devastating earthquake of 1923 which all but annihilated the city of Yokohama again found Nakada on a mission of mercy, seeking to speed relief to the disaster victims.

He advanced movements against government legislation which curbed religious freedom and firmly opposed the infamous shrine laws. At an interdenominational level, he sparked crusades which emphasized revival in the church, the return of Christ, and evangelical unity.

With the advent of radio, it was not surprising that Juji Nakada was the first Christian minister to speak over the air waves in Japan. The subject of that historic message: "The Oasis of Human Life."

The closing years of Nakada's life appear as an unfortunate anticlimax to a life so grandly used of God. They were years plagued by numerous physical complaints. But more unfortunate was his obsession with Japan Israelism—a strange teaching which held that the sole task of the church was to hasten the return of Christ by praying for the Jews' restoration to their homeland. The result was an eventual split within the Japan Holiness Church. Some maintain that Nakada's second wife, a strongly persuasive personality, influenced him in his peculiar views.

Was there some divine purpose underlying this regrettable turn of events that climaxed so rich a life? Some who have witnessed the Oriental's tendency to enshrine their heroes suggest that even the sad final note of Nakada's life may have been part of the design of the One who knows the beginning from the end.

On September 24, 1939, exactly 15 years after the death of Charles Cowman, Juji Nakada ended his earthly life. His second wife preceded him in death by ten days.

"Anyone can make people laugh," Nakada once pointed out to his son, "but few can make them weep." He was speaking of D. L. Moody, the man whose life had inspired him to cross the ocean in quest of the Holy Spirit. That Nakada, by the grace of God, succeeded in emulating his ideal is attested by thousands who under his ministry wept their way to repentance and faith in Christ.

3

Ernest Kilbourne

The few pictures available reveal a gentle man, unassuming and intensely sober behind steel-rimmed spectacles. His features are dignified by a high forehead and beard, trimmed in the fashion of the early 1900's.

Those who knew Ernest Kilbourne attest that he was a remarkable personality, chosen of God to share with Charles Cowman the burden of leadership in The Oriental Missionary Society. Although he demonstrated gifts as a writer, administrator, and missionary pioneer, it was his intimate walk with God that left the greatest impression upon the lives he touched.

"He was a man of true humility," wrote one who knew him well. "Yet to him, humility was not a negative cringing existence, but an active yielding to the power and presence of Almighty God whose purpose in the world, the greatest of all eternity, was to be accomplished by His own choosing through surrendered wills of redeemed human creatures."

This realization produced in Ernest Kilbourne an intriguing combination of qualities. Here was a man, humble to the point of self-effacement, who could, under the direction of the Holy Spirit, act with surprising boldness. On one occasion, he turned to a prominent church member who was living a "double life" with the seething rebuke, "Thou child of the devil!"

The work and lifelong friendship of Charles Cowman and Ernest

Kilbourne represented a magnificent merging of two minds and spirits. Their ministries so perfectly harmonized that Lettie Cowman could write of Ernest Kilbourne, "If the whole world had been searched throughout for one who would be a real fellow worker, another just like him could not have been found. Their lives were exact counterparts of each other. They moved together in perfect unison, they pulled together like the finest team...These two men made a lasting impression upon each other. They had the same burning love for Christ, the same compassion for the perishing, and were perfectly joined in one mind...They moved along the same line for a quarter of a century without a break in their unity of service."

Ernest Albert Kilbourne was born on March 13, 1865, in Niagara Falls, Ontario, within sound of the famous cataract. Two years later his parents moved west to the twin villages of Conestoga and Winterburn in Ontario. There his father established a general store, combined with a district telegraph and post office.

The Kilbournes, a deeply religious family for generations, had contributed a succession of sons to the ministry. Young Ernest attended the red brick Methodist church with his parents and sister, Mary. They sang the old unabridged hymns of John and Charles Wesley. And when Ernest and Mary wearied of the lengthy sermons, they scribbled notes in the hymnal. Forty-five years later, when the son of Ernest Kilbourne visited the historic family church, he was presented with a yellow hymnal still containing the notes scrawled in a childish hand.

Like Cowman, Ernest Kilbourne found in the magic of telegraphy an irresistible fascination. The wires that hummed their messages into the tiny telegraph office in an obscure Canadian town spoke to the young lad of an exciting world waiting to be discovered. By the time he was 14, he was a skilled operator earning his own money as an employee of the telegraph company. This was the first link in a chain of circumstances that would one day take Ernest Kilbourne to Chicago and a fateful meeting with Charles Cowman.

Ernest Kilbourne was not content in Conestoga long. While still in his teens, he left Ontario to take a position with the Western Union in the United States. Here was a growing company which offered unlimited opportunities for advancement to ambitious young men.

Once away from home, however, the urge to travel seized the

youth. Forgotten, for the time, was his religious upbringing and the teachings of the little Methodist church. He decided his future lay in journalism. Determined to become a writer, he set out to see the world. At the age of 21, he sailed from New York on a voyage that took him to Europe by way of Cape Town, South Africa, and on to Australia, New Zealand, and the Sandwich (Hawaiian) Islands. His horizons were being lifted, but his heart was far from God. Arriving back in San Francisco, he was caught up in the boisterous spirit of the thriving West. He found a job as a telegraph operator in Virginia City, Nevada—a brash silver-mining town peopled with rough miners and young fortune hunters.

Ernest did not stay in Virginia City long. But he remained long enough to meet and fall in love with a sweet Catholic girl who became his wife and later shared his faith in Jesus Christ. A jovial person blessed with an unfailing sense of humor, she endeared herself to all she met. Through many difficult years she proved a good homemaker, mother, and helpmeet.

There was little future for a telegraph operator in the remote western outpost of Virginia City. Ernest Kilbourne requested a transfer to Chicago and the city's huge central telegraph office. Energetic and intensely ambitious, he was soon receiving regular promotions. In a relatively short time, he found himself in the responsible position of a divisional chief. He, along with another man, had almost 1,000 operators working under their supervision. The other man was Charles Cowman.

From the outset, Cowman and Kilbourne had much in common. Both men had outstanding capabilities; both bent their energies to achieve success, wealth, and prominence in the business and social world. Neither had time for religion.

With Charles Cowman's sudden return to God, it was natural that he should turn to his closest friend, Ernest Kilbourne, in his first soul-winning effort. The encounter ended with Cowman convinced that he had failed miserably in his initial witness for his Lord. But at that time he knew little of the means or methods of the Holy Spirit.

The next morning, Ernest Kilbourne met the young wire chief with what must have been an astonishing greeting. "Charles," he announced, "I did what you told me to do last night, and I have given my heart to Jesus Christ." The simple statement described an immutable transaction that left Ernest Kilbourne's soul and life purpose forever changed. The decision was accompanied by an utter commitment of his life to Christ—a commitment from which he never withdrew.

Now Ernest Kilbourne's every energy and ambition was directed Godward. Action followed swiftly on the heels of decision. He joined the Grace Methodist Church and enrolled in the Moody Bible Institute for night classes.

Cowman and Kilbourne invested their spare time in a variety of soul-winning activities. They witnessed on the streets, in parks, and to the derelicts that frequented mission halls. Everywhere they distributed gospel tracts. On the way home after their late shift, they would place tracts in all the mailboxes along the streets they passed.

The two men looked on the telegraph office as their divinely appointed field of service. Systematically, with wisdom and spiritual tact, they confronted their colleagues with the claims of Jesus Christ. An ever-enlarging group of converts in the telegraph office gave rise to an organization designed to conserve the fruits and provide a channel for witness. In 1894 the Telegraphers Mission Band was formed. It grew into an international fellowship of telegraphers who sought to win their fellow operators everywhere to Christ. From this organization emerged the beginnings of The Oriental Missionary Society.

The Christian concern that expressed itself in Ernest Kilbourne's tireless soul-winning efforts needed only a spark to set it ablaze with missionary passion for the unreached millions in foreign lands. Dr. A. B. Simpson, founder of the Christian and Missionary Alliance, provided that spark. A great missionary convention at which Simpson was the principal speaker left both Cowman and Kilbourne with a missionary vision that was unabated until their deaths.

With new vision came a dramatic and distinct call to go to the Orient as a faith missionary. At this time, Kilbourne received a revelation of unusual clarity and significance. He saw a great highway bridge arching across the Pacific Ocean to Japan. From Japan, a span of the bridge reached Korea, and from Korea a third link touched China. From China, the great highway seemed to extend directly to heaven. In the years that followed, Ernest Kilbourne would witness the fulfillment of this vision in every detail.

Kilbourne now began a lifetime of intercession for the Orient. He bought a large map. In prayer he placed his hands on the countries of Asia, visualizing their teeming, unreached populations. Long hours on his knees over the map of Japan impressed on his mind not only the names of scores of towns and villages, but also an amazing knowledge of the intricate topography of the islands.

Charles and Lettie Cowman sailed for Japan in 1901, leaving Ernest Kilbourne in charge of the Telegraphers Mission Band. Kilbourne longed to be with his beloved colleague in Tokyo, but a promise to God kept him in Chicago. During and after a previous employment with a railway company, he had misused a free pass which had been granted him. At his conversion, he had promised he would make complete financial restitution to his former employers. Ernest Kilbourne determined that promise should be kept before he had any business serving God on foreign soil.

A year later, the last of the money had been repaid. Ernest Kilbourne, with his wife and family, made plans to join the Cowmans in Japan. A church where they had frequently attended enthusiastically pledged their full support. Encouraged by this demonstration of love, they started for San Francisco where they were to find booking on a ship for Japan.

In San Francisco they received distressing news in the form of a telegram from the church that had pledged to stand behind them. Since their departure, the congregation had split into factions; the chairman of the board regretted to inform them that "the pledge of support is cancelled."

If the news came as a blow to Ernest Kilbourne, he accepted it as a challenge of faith. "I am so certain God wants us in Japan," he said to his wife, "I could start walking on water. "

This unshakable confidence in God was ever the hallmark of Ernest Kilbourne. "Faith grows amid storms, " he later wrote in an article that reveals a keen insight into the nature of faith. "Faith is that Godgiven faculty which, when exercised, brings the unseen into plain view, and by which the impossible things are made possible ... but it grows amid storms; that is, where there are disturbances in the spiritual atmosphere. Storms are caused by conflicts of elements, and the storms of the world are conflicts of hostile elements. In such an atmosphere, faith finds its most productive soil; in such an element, it comes more quickly to full fruition. The staunchest tree is not found in the shelter of the forest, but out in the open where the winds from every quarter beat upon it and bend it and twist it until it becomes a giant in stature...amid storms—right in the midst where it is fiercest. You may shrink back from the ordeal of a fierce storm or trial, but go in! God is there to meet you in the center of all your trials and to whisper His secrets which will make you come forth with a shining face and an indomitable faith that all the demons of hell shall never afterwards cause to waver.''

The Kilbournes eventually found passage on the *Nippon Maru,* a Japanese ship equipped with sails to supplement steam power and economize on coal. During the first four days of the tedious 24-day crossing, the vessel slowly rocked its way through a violent storm. Below deck, in far-from-commodious fourth class quarters, the Kilbournes, suffering from their first experience with seasickness, took to their bunks.

Ernest Kilbourne determined that the long weeks on the ocean should not be wasted time. Why wait until his arrival in Japan to begin missionary work; there were Japanese all around him that needed Christ. He joined the ship's crew at mealtime as they squatted in a circle on their heels. While they deftly plied their chopsticks, he spoke to them of Jesus Christ.

It was raining the day the *Nippon Maru* dropped anchor at the port of Yokohama. The month was August, 1902. The final hazard of disembarking climaxed the long comfortless voyage. Limited harbor facilities required that the ship anchor out in the bay. With the other passengers, the Kilbournes boarded a smoky tug. From the tug, they transferred to bobbing sampans which ferried them to land.

Ashore, the Cowmans with a group of Japanese Christians extended a warm welcome to the tired travelers. The last leg of the journey was a ride on a jolting narrow gauge railroad to Tokyo station. There they climbed into picturesque jinrickishas to be hustled through the crowded streets to the Cowmans' home. The Kilbournes were at last in Japan. Ernest looked in his wallet—empty of all but a five dollar bill—and praised God.

In order to more effectively concentrate on the study of the Japanese language, Ernest Kilbourne requested to live in a native home in a small town outside Tokyo. Cowman agreed to this, sending him off with the advice, ''Remember, nothing but study. Get the language and don't get involved in preaching and meetings. Nothing is to hinder your progress in the language."

The family located in a native farmhouse with a typical thatched roof. There they adapted to life, Japanese style. If the experience was a new one for them, their neighbors hardly knew what to think of it. Who ever heard of Americans living under a thatched roof like the Japanese? Some were suspicious. Everyone was curious.

Soon word got around that townsfolk were welcome at the foreigners' home. Privacy was a forgotten luxury for the Kilbournes. Both the back and front doors were left open to inquisitive neighbors intent on seeing for themselves how the foreigners lived. Before long they were asking about the "new religion."

Inevitably the "home" became a "church." New believers needed nourishment. Services were held, often as many as fourteen a week. The Kilbournes were learning Japanese and Japanese were learning about Christ. Many had found Him as Savior.

Among those who visited the new home were keen young men whom Ernest Kilbourne was not slow to claim for the Master. Seven of these men were destined to serve as key leaders in the growing Japan Holiness Church. Their lives, like those of many others, stand as enduring monuments to Ernest Kilbourne's conviction that every soul has vast possibilities of usefulness in the kingdom of God. Once asked why he had been so successful in directing young lives into the service of Jesus Christ, he replied, "Every soul it is my joy to lead to Christ, I see as a potential Christian worker. I pray and labor for them until I see God's full will accomplished in their lives."

With Cowman, Kilbourne felt a growing certainty that the missionaries' prime task was to train nationals. In his tribute to Charles Cowman, he describes the process by which God's plan came to them:

"I can hear Brother Cowman pouring out his heart to God for missionaries. One hundred missionaries was the burden of his prayer. Those were days when we thought of missionaries as white folks, and God's large purpose and plan had not penetrated our minds. . . Those prayers were answered, though not as we thought. White folks? Yes, but not many. God's thought was not our thought, at least not then. And better than we knew, God was answering. That answer has meant a thousand missionaries: Japanese, Korean, Chinese. And as we look back now, we see how much better than we realized, God answers prayer.''

In his booklet entitled, ''The Story of a Mission,'' he wrote, ''The native ministry is the solution. We appreciate the fact that if a missionary can train say five Japanese and get them filled with the Holy Spirit and then have them preaching in three or four years, he will have multiplied himself by five, for he himself must spend the three or four years studying the language before he can do the work he came to do. So we claim that a Bible training school is the quickest method of solving the great question of saving the soul of Japan.''

Ten years after his arrival in Japan, Ernest Kilbourne and Charles Cowman became convinced that their task was to literally fulfill the great commission in Japan by taking the gospel of Christ to the 10,300,000 homes of the land. Nothing of this sort had ever been accomplished in the history of modern missions, and the task loomed before them like an enormous mountain.

In the biography of Charles Cowman, Kilbourne discloses their feelings the morning God showed them the pattern for the first Great Village Campaign:

'' 'Impossible,' the enemy insistently whispered. Think of the millions of homes in this empire of 60,000,000 people; just think of the congested cities with their interminable alleys; just think of the great mountains everywhere to be crossed; just think of transporting the literature to the innumerable villages of the far interior; just think of the thousands of homes hidden in the fastness of the snow-clad mountains; just think of the impassable roads and paths to be traversed; just think of the inhospitable reception one must meet among fanatical idolators; just think of the lack of hotel accommodations to be found for the workers in the country districts and especially in the mountainous parts.''

Ernest Kilbourne's response to the challenge was typical. He took five dollars from his pocket—all the money he had—and laid it on an open Bible, across the verse, ''Go ye into all the world, and preach the gospel to every creature.'' In doing so he acted in consistency with a long-established life principle which held, ''I am God's, and everything I have belongs to Him as well.''

Years before he had renounced with glad abandon all but the bare necessities of life. He exchanged his expensive gold watch for a cheap one.

The savings went to missions. He persuaded his wife to sacrifice her wedding ring for the same cause. A generous life insurance policy was dropped; he withdrew from a costly mutual assistance organization.

"He was a man of self-denial," testified a missionary co-worker. "When he held a responsible position in the telegraph company, he had a full wardrobe; but as a missionary he usually owned but one suit of clothes. During the week he wore it unbuttoned; on Sundays he buttoned it to effect a change."

Though they often lived on the margin of poverty, the Kilbournes never lost their appreciation for the beautiful. One day while entertaining guests at tea, he turned to his wife, addressing her with a favorite term of affection, "Pet," he said, "we've always loved nice chinaware, but maybe we'll have our desire at the Marriage Supper of the Lamb."

Ernest Kilbourne, whose youthful ambitions had led him into a short-lived career as a writer, was not slow to grasp the unlimited possibilities of a gospel literature ministry in a land that boasted the highest literacy rate in the world.

"It is not an unusual thing," he reported, "for us to pass out 50,000 or more tracts in one afternoon's work among the dense crowds gathered at some temple on a festival day in Tokyo, where hundreds of thousands of people are participating."

"Satan is doing his best to flood this empire with poisonous literature...a visit to the bookstores reveals the awful fact that thousands of Japan's young men are absorbing this poison to such an extent that the coming generation bids fair to outrival France in her bloody days of Voltairism.

"To offset this, there is a need of thousands of dollars to scatter, free of charge, red-hot salvation literature throughout the land."

In time, a print shop was opened, a press installed, and a tide of gospel literature released from the small center into every province of Japan. Fruits from this ministry remain to this day.

As an author, Kilbourne was immensely effective. His style was direct, sometimes abrupt, but always penetrating. "The writings of Ernest A. Kilbourne," said the noted evangelist and educator, H. C. Morrison, "have stirred my soul more than any writings next to the Bible itself."

His pen, dipped in holy fire, was touched to many a lethargic church, setting it ablaze with missionary concern. Always he appealed to the Scriptures as his authority, and every message is weighted with a sense of responsibility for immortal souls.

"It is an awful fact," he wrote in one of his many editorials published in *Electric Messages* (now *The Missionary Standard*), "that man has the power to disobey God. Moreover, he not only has the power to do so, but he uses that power; he does disobey and works fearful disaster to his own soul and to others. . . The child of God has power to thwart his Father's plan and purpose in the earth by his indifference and disobedience. Not that it is in his heart to do so, but often through neglect and ignorance he hinders and even thwarts God's purposes for himself and others. This is especially true concerning the evangelization of the world.

"His 'Go ye' to men is no less irrevocable and unalterable than the laws that hold the universe together, and the disaster that has already ensued from the neglect and disobedience has wrecked and ruined whole nations for centuries, so that myriads of heathen have been lost because of a disloyal church."

The first span of the arching bridge that appeared in the vision of Ernest Kilbourne had been crossed. The second was to lead him to Korea, "The Land of the Morning Calm," undoubtedly the ripest mission field of this day.

First contact with Korea was established when two Korean pastors appeared at the Tokyo Bible School. They wore outlandish bloomer-type trousers and horsehair hats. From Juji Nakada, they had learned of the unique training center and were impressed that God was directing them there for further preparation. Soon others from Korea joined them seeking practical instruction in a soul-winning ministry and a personal experience of the filling of the Holy Spirit.

Cowman and Kilbourne interpreted this as God's signal to advance into the long-neglected land of Korea. The pattern so blessed of God in Japan would be the plan for the work in Korea as well. The Rev. John Thomas, a popular and dynamic Welsh evangelist, was called to join hands with Ernest Kilbourne in the pioneer venture.

Kilbourne, who had already seen how God can work to "bring into being things that are not," was confident that in Korea, too, He would pay for all He had ordered. Simply trusting God for provision of the funds, they secured a property in downtown Seoul and established a Bible training center at the strategic location. From the institute, pastors were sent out to plant the Church of Jesus Christ.

The Every Creature Crusade, so effective in Japan, was established in Korea. Again, God blessed the contagious witness of hot-hearted Christians as they carried the Word of Life from house to house until three-fourths of the population of 30,000,000 had been reached with the gospel.

The growth of the church in Korea can only be described as phenomenal. Its history is a veritable repetition of the Acts of the Apostles. Decades of persecution and martyrdom climaxed by the communist massacre of thousands of Christians in the early 1950's only spurred the church in its relentless advance. Throughout the world, the church of Korea is known as "The Miracle Church." Today (1969), the OMS has 600 churches in Korea with a total of 165,553 believers.

In 1931, when the OMS church in Japan became entirely self-supporting, the headquarters of the Society was moved to Korea. Here Ernest Kilbourne extended to the people of Korea the same warmth and generous spirit that had won him so large a place in the hearts of the Japanese. Korean Christians still speak of him in terms of loving respect and recall with gratitude his sacrificial spirit.

Missionaries and nationals who labored with Ernest Kilbourne were most impressed by his tireless life of prayer. "I can still see E. A. Kilbourne," a fellow missionary recalls, "as he would pace back and forth on the porch of the mission home after the lunch hour in communion with his Lord. No napping after lunch for Brother Kilbourne. He chose the after-lunch period because at that time of the day there were fewer disturbances; he was always seen walking back and forth. We knew he was interceding for us in a growing work."

For him, prayer was no ethereal exercise. It was the great imperative of the Christian life. It was grappling with realities. His writings were punctuated with the urgent query, "Are you praying? Beloved, the secret is prayer."

Those who heard him pray remember his simple childlike faith. He dared ask God for practical needs—for strength for the day, for health. A friend traveling with Kilbourne recorded, "He daily drew his strength from the Lord. On several occasions while traveling together as we had our morning devotions, he would beseech the Lord for strength for the day. He believed in the Lord for the body and the body for the Lord. And in the confidence that his life was united to Christ's life, he trusted for the outflow of His life into his life, thus quickening him for each day.''

From the time of his conversion he had learned of the privilege of the Christian in taking the Lord to be his ''Great Physician,'' and throughout his Christian life he never had to call on the help of a doctor. He expressed the secret of his continuing good health in his daily conscious committing of his bodily health to the Lord. ''It is far more practical and glorifying to God,'' he once said, ''to be divinely kept in daily health than to have to call on the Lord for divine healing after being overcome by illness.''

In 1907, Cowman and Kilbourne went to Shanghai, China, to attend a centennial conference commemorating the coming of Robert Morrison to that land. In the quiet of their separate rooms, God revealed to both men that The Oriental Missionary Society was to open work in China. ''That day in 1907,'' said Kilbourne, ''in a hotel in Shanghai, Brother Cowman and I were definitely called to that field. Although years of inaction passed, that vision ever held and never dimmed; contrariwise, it brightened.''

One year before the OMS entered China, Charles Cowman was called to be with his Lord. At his bedside he committed to his lifelong friend the burden of the Society's leadership. It would remain to Ernest Kilbourne to fulfill the call to China received almost 20 years earlier. For him, it would mark the completion of the third span of the arching bridge—the link God had shown him, which would stretch from Korea to China.

China was in a state of upheaval in 1925 when Ernest Kilbourne and a vanguard of missionaries arrived in Shanghai to initiate the new work. They had apparently chosen a singularly inopportune time to enter this field. Everything indicated that the venture was a folly. The missionary treasury was empty. And worse, the country was in the throes of civil uprisings with ominous antichristian overtones. Missionaries were leaving by the hundreds, and some predicted that Christianity in China would be set back 100 years.

Shanghai was aswarm with fleeing missionaries. Hotels and hostels were so crowded some were obliged to sleep in hallways and bathrooms. Rough board bunks were being installed in out-going freighters to accommodate the departing passengers.

A veteran missionary, speaking to some 20 Christian workers who were housed temporarily in a YMCA washroom, expressed what many were thinking. "The Oriental Missionary Society starting a work in China at a time like this?" he exclaimed. "You must be fools." Ironically, it was this same missionary whose home was rented by the OMS, making it the first headquarters for the work in China.

Contrary to the doleful predictions, Kilbourne and his party discovered that political and civil uncertainty had left the people hungry for spiritual reality. There was an eager response to the gospel, especially among the young people of Shanghai.

A spacious site was located and a training center built while OMS missionaries were provided rent-free accommodations at the Bethel Mission—a work established by two intrepid women of God, Dr. Mary Stone and Miss Jennie Hughes.

God prospered The Oriental Missionary Society in China. Three Bible schools turned out scores of Spirit-filled pastors and evangelists until the Bamboo Curtain fell in 1949. Many of the graduates have paid for their faith with their blood; others, at the risk of their lives, continue a valiant witness for their Lord.

While still in the process of establishing the first training center, God led Ernest Kilbourne in what may have been the most important spiritual contact of his ministry. One of the co-workers at the Bethel Mission was Andrew Gih, a young man with exceptional abilities. Returning from a service with Andrew Gih one afternoon, Kilbourne explained to the lad the scriptural basis for the truly victorious life through the filling of the Holy Spirit. He found in the youth a soul God had been preparing for just such instruction. There in the crowded bus, the two men bowed in prayer and Andrew Gih entered into the glorious experience that made of him a dynamic and vastly influential servant of God. Today he is internationally recognized as one of the most effective evangelists Asia has ever produced.

It was no accident that Ernest Kilbourne was God's instrument to reveal to Andrew Gih the nature and work of the Holy Spirit in the life of the believer. Kilbourne knew from personal experience what could happen to the weak and timid when possessed by the Spirit of God. His own solemn sense of dependence on God was always coupled with an audacious confidence in what the Holy Spirit could accomplish through human instruments when He had control of them.

"Soul-saving is not hard work for the Spirit-filled worker," he wrote. "God takes the weak folk and makes them strong. He takes unstable ones and makes them constant. . . we may only be made thus by the baptism of the Holy Ghost and fire which exterminates all indifferences to God's purpose and plants in us a constraining love to obey God."

The constraining love which dictated every action of Ernest Kilbourne's life is especially apparent in his relationships with his fellow workers. One remembers that "he evidenced confidence in people's ability. He appointed them to places of responsibility and stood back of them in difficulty. . . . He was a trusting man. He accepted people for what they professed to be and was keenly disappointed when anyone let him down and did not live up to the confidence he had placed in them; he was always eager to do whatever he could do to please others and this was manifest in innumerable ways."

Never one to hold a grudge, he was once heard to remark, "Many people bury the hatchet with the handle sticking out." A missionary remembers that once when Ernest Kilbourne had been wronged, he so completely forgot the incident that not only did he fail to recall the perpetrator of the wrong, but he could not remember the wrong itself. In the flyleaf of the Bible which he gave his son, he penned the following:

> Keep thine own quiet way;
> Mind not what folk may say,
> God is the judge,
> Not they.

The verse seemed to sum up his entire manner of life. In all, he sought only the approval of God.

On April 13, 1928, Ernest Kilbourne was ready to cross the final span of the great bridge he saw in the vision years before. He was about to enter into the presence of the Lord he loved so well and served so faithfully. His death of a cerebral hemorrhage came so suddenly friends compared it to Enoch's experience: He "walked with God: and he was not; for God took him."

A few hours before his passing, he wrote a letter to all his missionary associates. In it he praised God that he had no personal bank account and that he did not own a square foot of property. Yet God had privileged him to have millions of dollars pass through his hands for the great missionary cause for which he lived and died.

When the word of his death reached Japan, a great memorial service was held at which 2,000 Japanese were present. The seven leaders who had found Christ in Kilbourne's first home in the Orient passed through the congregation accepting a love offering to be sent to the bereaved Mother Kilbourne.

Although Ernest Kilbourne died with only $80 to his name, he left behind a priceless legacy. His family, to whom he left no estate, insurance, or wealth has been blessed by the Father to whom he so joyfully entrusted them. Two generations of Kilbournes followed his noble example, investing their lives in missionary service. A fourth generation of Kilbournes is presently in training for Christian service.

Ernest Kilbourne lives on in the testimonies of faithful Christians who bear the name of Jesus Christ in Japan, Korea, and China. His self-effacing life of devotion to his Master forever recalls the beautiful paradox of the servant of God: ''as poor, yet making many rich; as having nothing, and yet possessing all things.''

4

Lettie B. Cowman

In a small Korean home a lone missionary, sick in body and far from loved ones, was facing the quiet agony of despair accompanied by a feeling of utter uselessness. He turned to a small volume of devotional readings which had recently been given him.

"The book opened my eyes," he said. "From its pages, there came a fresh understanding of God's purposes. Defeat was transformed into victory. In place of sorrow and frustration came great joy."

The missionary was but one of generations of sufferers who have been ministered to by *Streams in the Desert,* a book that has often been called "the best-loved devotional of our time." The secret of this remarkable book cannot be understood apart from the life of the author, who through the shock and astonishment of her own deep grief gradually gained rich insights into the methods and purposes of God. She was Mrs. Lettie B. Cowman, who after the passing of her husband served for many years as president of The Oriental Missionary Society.

A missionary executive, an internationally-known speaker, the organizer of gospel distribution missions, Mrs. Cowman will be remembered most as an apostle of consolation. As long as there exists spiritual need, physical pain, and the torment of unanswered questions, her sacred collections will minister their sweet fragrances and God's people will be blessed. The life of Mrs. Lettie Cowman will remain a great standard of faith and forever an illustration of the sufficiency of divine grace in the midst of suffering.

Lettie Burd Cowman was born to Isaac and Margaret Burd in Afton, Iowa, on March 3, 1870. This life that was to be marked by sacrifice had its improbable beginning amid conspicuous plenty. Although Lettie's parents had come to the frontier state as pioneers, their life savings sewn into their garments, Mr. Burd was not long in establishing himself as a successful banker. Soon his generous income made possible comforts quite foreign to the life of the average frontiersman. The Burd home was distinguished by an atmosphere of culture. Lettie was early surrounded with art, literature, and music. It was a comfortable life which offered abundance and made few demands—the kind of life which sufficiently indulged in may leave the soul with little taste for the way of the Cross. Lettie later acknowledged, "In a sense, Charles Cowman was my savior. He saved me from the life of wealth, leisure, and plenty."

Lettie was the last of the Burd children, arriving on the scene after all of her brothers and sisters had left home. Continually in the presence of adults, she matured rapidly and beyond her years. To fill the emptiness of her child's world she turned for companionship to the world of books, music, and nature, developing a lifelong appreciation for these things. Sensitive to beauty, she never ceased to look with genuine awe at the magnificence of a sunrise or marvel at the miracle of a budding rose.

Relationships destined to have the most profound effect upon human lives often begin with no more than a casual encounter. "Today I met a dear lad at the railway station," Mrs. Burd announced one morning. "He seemed so clean and fine, but with an air of loneliness about him. I thought he needed some mothering, so I invited him to the house." The boy's name was Charles Cowman. Just a youth, he had recently left home to take a job with the Western Union Telegraph Company. Soon Charles was making regular visits to the Burd estate.

Between the lonely banker's daughter and the young telegrapher far from home there developed a friendship that filled deep vacancies in both lives. Lettie's parents, however, made it painfully apparent that they regarded the deepening friendship with something less than approval. It was with considerable relief that they received word of Charles' transfer to a distant telegraph office. Certainly the separation would bring a welcome termination to the teenage romance, they reasoned. Charles, however, had other plans. Before leaving he drew Lettie aside to a favorite meeting place by the lake; there he declared in no uncertain terms his intentions. Her response was immediate and eager. "I love you, Charles," she stated simply. "I promise to wait for you."

While Lettie solemnly kept her pledge to Charles, her parents were devising a scheme that provided a two-fold advantage. Why not send Lettie to Vienna to pursue her musical interests? Her teacher had already proposed a musical career for the girl. More than that, the term abroad would make the continuation of the stubborn friendship almost hopelessly impractical. The plan was advanced with considerable fervor. Large sums were spent on clothes and appropriate accessories. But the Burds' designs were in the end thwarted by the adamant will of their daughter. After all, had she not promised?

Lettie was blossoming into womanhood. Talented, gay, creative, with a laugh like the light tinkle of a bell, it was obvious to all that the banker's daughter was an unusually attractive and desirable young lady. Young men with the proper social rank and pedigree to satisfy the Burds pursued Lettie with ardor. One, an officer in Mr. Burd's bank, was particularly acceptable to them. He offered to surround Lettie with the comforts to which she was accustomed and guarantee her considerable financial security.

But the parents' enthusiasm for the match was not shared by Lettie. A second time, the ambitions of well-meaning parents were frustrated by the quiet determination of this young woman who would not take lightly her pledge.

At the age of 21, Charles Cowman returned to the Burd estate. Behind him now were five years of outstanding service with the Western Union Telegraph Company. He came back with a new confidence well earned. Hardly out of his teens, he had been appointed manager of the telegraph office in Glenwood Springs, Colorado. Although he could not offer Lettie wealth or the life of the drawing room to which she was accustomed, he promised her reasonable security and bright prospects for the future.

Witnessing the reunion of the young sweethearts, the Burds bowed before the inevitable. On June 18, 1889, in the Methodist Church of Afton, Iowa, Lettie Burd and Charles Cowman entered into a union which only God could have planned. The parents, smiling through their disappointment, gave the couple their blessing and a beautiful reception.

The Cowmans' first home was in Glenwood Springs, Colorado, high amid the towering grandeur of the Rocky Mountains. Magnificent as the scenery was, the altitude soon proved too high for Lettie's heart. Once, at the point of death, God spared her life in answer to Charles' desperate prayer. Shortly thereafter, they moved to Chicago where Charles rapidly advanced to the position of Western Union Division Chief with some fifty operators under his supervision. Now they enjoyed a generous income, and Charles was able to provide Lettie with some of the comforts which she had known earlier. Frequently, they were found at the opera or at some prestigious social event.

"What did an opera star have to gain by abandoning a promising career in favor of the vagrant life of a gospel singer—to sing to restless children and church people, most of whom were unable to fully appreciate her talents?"

The question must have probed the soul of Lettie Cowman as she sat in the Grace Methodist Church, struck by the exceptional quality of the artist's voice. A handbill brought to their door earlier that week had induced her to come. "Opera singer to appear in concert at Grace Methodist Church," it had announced.

Not just an ordinary opera singer, Lettie decided as she listened. The voice revealed something more than artistry; it exuded a certain quality of joy, hardly containable, a kind of ecstacy quite foreign to anything Lettie had ever known. What had this woman discovered? What was it that induced her to so heartily relinquish the very things that she and Charles had set their hearts on? All in all, the service was a disturbing experience, and Lettie Cowman resolved not to return.

Nevertheless, the following evening at seven o'clock, Lettie, half annoyed with herself, was seated in the red brick sanctuary of the Grace Methodist Church. Music, the thing that had always charmed her, had now brought a sudden discord into her life. What was it in the singer's voice that so troubled her, making her keenly conscious of gnawing dissatisfaction?

One night after the concert, an invitation was given. A group of children surged to the front to "give their hearts to Jesus." A ten-year-old boy arose with a glowing face to declare, "I have found sweet peace in my heart."

A woman seated next to Lettie Cowman turned to her and asked pointedly, "Are you serving the Lord?"

"No," came the straightforward reply, "I am serving the world and myself."

"Why don't you give yourself to Jesus?"

"But I don't know how."

"I'll go with you."

A hand slipped into Lettie's and she was guided down the long aisle to the place of prayer. There, kneeling at the lower altar amid a cluster of children, a proud woman prayed a prayer of the penitent. The transaction was immediate and complete.

"I will never be able to explain it," she said, "but from that moment, I belonged to the Lord." The new life had taken root in her soul. Later when someone asked if she had always been of a religious nature and if she had followed God from earliest childhood, she quickly answered, "No, until I was converted I was full of the world, the flesh, and the devil."

Charles Cowman noted that "the change in my wife which immediately followed was a great surprise to me, for she at once separated herself from the world and testified that she was genuinely converted."

Impressed by the change as he was, Charles was, nevertheless, far from enthusiastic about his wife's sudden interest in religious matters. In the circles in which they now moved, this brand of religion was all but unmentionable. People who talked openly of a personal relationship with Christ were quickly dismissed as fanatics. But perhaps, more than anything else, Lettie's glowing testimony for her Saviour came to Charles as an uncomfortable reminder of a once-precious childhood experience at an altar and a more recent vow made to God at the bedside of his dying wife.

But nothing Charles could say would dissuade Lettie from her sacred commitment. With the same quiet resolve she had shown in keeping her love pledge to him despite parental disapproval, she now kept a higher promise. One Sunday morning she stood alone at the front of the 600-member Grace Methodist Church to take the vows of membership.

That Christmas, Charles, always the considerate husband, chose what he sensed was an appropriate gift for his wife—a Bible. Certainly the choice would please her, he reasoned. On the fly leaf he wrote briefly, "Lettie Burd Cowman, from her husband. Christmas, 1893." It was the first of many treasured Bibles whose thumb-worn penciled pages remain to this day as chronicles of a woman's ever-deepening relationship with her Lord.

One evening Charles came home to present Lettie with tickets and an invitation to a performance of the grand opera. Lettie's polite refusal confirmed Charles' fears. With his wife's drastically altered life, strong ties of mutual interest and ambition which had once bound them so closely had fallen away. In their place seemed to have come an ever-widening gulf. The consciousness of it came with a stab of pain. That evening he went to the opera alone but returned early with the complaint that the music was poor and the story inferior.

Soon after, a week of special meetings was scheduled at the Grace Methodist Church. Yielding to his wife's urgings, Charles consented to attend one Sunday evening. It was a night they would both remember and thank God for. By the time they returned that evening, the Holy Spirit had crushed the ambitious young telegraph executive. In their home, Charles fell to his knees and with characteristic wholeheartedness presented himself to God. It was Lettie Cowman's greatest triumph.

For Charles and Lettie the night marked a blissful reunion. They were one again—one in Christ. It was a wedding of hearts and spirits destined to glorify God and extend the gospel to waiting continents.

Bible study, church attendance, and personal witnessing became consuming interests in the lives of the Cowmans. Their home, always a happy one, now became a center of Christian activity and a source of inspiration. And one by one, Charles was winning fellow telegraphers to Christ.

Yet it took a missionary convention at the Moody Church in Chicago and an appeal by world missionary leader, A.B. Simpson (founder of the Christian and Missionary Alliance), to dramatically arouse the couple to a consideration of the needs of a waiting world far beyond the telegraph office or the Chicago "Little Hell" slums where Charles regularly spent Sunday evenings witnessing. At Simpson's call for volunteers for foreign service, Charles turned to his wife with a resolve she well understood. "This means you and me," he said simply.

At first the missionary volunteers were drawn to India, but their hopes were disappointed when doctors refused to give Lettie a clean bill of health, declaring that her body was too frail to withstand the torturous tropical climate. There seemed nothing to do but wait further direction. Meanwhile, they set about to prepare themselves for whatever ministry God might have for them. Both enrolled as students in the Moody Bible Training Institute.

No doubt it was in God's plan that the Cowmans were not immediately accepted as missionary candidates. The months of waiting provided time and opportunity for a thorough examination of the soul life. Lettie, reared in comfort and accustomed to plenty, had long been attached to the amusements of the world. She was to discover that before the soul can be beautified with spiritual graces, it must first be stripped of worldly ornaments and trifling loves that sap the spiritual life and leave the heart divided against itself. Gradually under the tutorship of the Holy Spirit this was to be accomplished.

For years Lettie had been a devotee of light fiction. "A harmless diversion, " she would have described it. Now, however, there merged a growing uneasiness. Such reading matter, she concluded, was blunting the keen edge of her Christian witness and spoiling her taste for the Word of God. Finally she confided to her diary, "I cannot continue to have companionship with the blessed Trinity while reading these novels." Directly she consigned volume after volume to the fire.

If this decision was dramatic, it was not impulsive. The surrender was irrevocable and complete. Henceforth her mind would be fed exclusively on the Word of God and such writings as shed light on the Scriptures. She had made her choice. Narrow? Some dolefully suggested that she was removing from reality, isolating herself in the drab world of religion. But what did they know of the ever-widening vistas of divine truth that fling themselves before the seeker with irresistible appeal? Charles and Lettie had chosen to immerse themselves in the Book. It would be their meat and drink. Sensitivities tuned, they learned to draw from this great source rich satisfactions, even in the time of famine.

There were other alterations that God was making in the life of Lettie Cowman. One morning as she sat down at the piano, her eyes fell upon a sheaf of music—popular tunes, opera music, dance songs. Often this music had brought her pleasant distraction; the lilting melodies had occupied many an hour and often her fingers had plucked the sensuous chords from the piano with a certain gay abandon. But now this music had turned bittersweet. With pleasure came also the now-familiar uneasiness. Could it be that this, too, would have to be placed at the foot of the Cross? Looking again at the orderly pile atop the polished piano she heard, "Does all this glorify your Lord?" In an instant the decision was made. These, too, like trinkets now useless and cumbersome, must be dropped away.

During this period, the work of God in the life of Lettie Cowman was twofold in nature. Not only was her life being stripped for service, she was at the same time being equipped for service. Her natural timidity and reticence to attempt public ministry was gradually surrendered. In its place, God gave her unusual abilities as a public speaker. Lettie Cowman could move audiences with words. Beginning first with children's meetings, then youth services—dramatic and often illustrated—she gained confidence and poise. People remembered her vivid presentations. Years later a youth worker at a camp recalled, "The young people were crazy about her. She kept us on the edge of our seats for two hours. While she was speaking, we seemed to lose all consciousness of time."

With steady progress in the spiritual life came blessing and daily enrichment. Yet Lettie was not satisfied. She had received clear instruction regarding the work of the Holy Ghost. Now she longed for the infilling of the Spirit with the accompanying cleansing and empowering for service.

"One morning I rose at four o'clock," she later recalled. "I wanted to pray and do some searching of the Word. Just as I knelt I felt an unseen Presence so near me I looked up to see who was there. I could not utter a word, but just felt hushed in that glorious Presence. A sweet rest filled my being, and I knew that the Holy Spirit had come to abide forever. Nothing has ever been able to shake the experience of that hour alone with God. For 21 years He has kept me through smooth ways and thorny paths, in battles and victories, in homeland and among the heathen and this morning as I pen this testimony the witness still is in my heart that the 'blood of Jesus cleanseth me from all sin.' His will is the sweetest thing on earth.''

That morning encounter remained in her life, not as an isolated attainment, but the basis of a daily and ever-deepening relationship with the Saviour. Her emphasis was never on past experience, but rather, ''God spoke to me this morning through His Word.'' Her Bibles eloquently witness a living relationship with God; the margins overflow with daily bulletins from heaven. One who made a careful study of her Bibles noted that ''there is scarcely a page from Genesis to Revelation which has not been marked. In addition, there are brief outlines, quotations, dates, names, places.'' The materials from these Bibles would fill a volume. Lettie Cowman loved God's Word. She approached the Book with the reverent attitude of a listener, heart attuned to catch whispers of love, instruction, encouragement. Or compare her to a skillful miner working a fabulous lode from which he daily drew shiny nuggets or whole veins of precious metal.

By the turn of the century, the years of preparation were nearing completion. Of the deep inner work in two lives, God was able to say, ''It is well; now they may go.'' One Saturday morning, August 11, 1900, at 10:30 a.m., Charles received the call to Japan. But what of his wife? Would she now be willing and ready for a sudden alteration in their way of life? Would her dedication be good for that remote Oriental empire? He need not have worried. ''Six weeks ago while I was alone,'' she told her husband after he had announced his call, ''God spoke to me about going to Japan. I have kept it hidden in my heart waiting the right moment to tell you.''

To the average American, the pre-jet world of Japan was little more than an exotic name—a quaint little island inhabited by small but friendly people, located somewhere in the general direction of China. In the Japan of 1901, the presence of white faces drew curious stares, even in the heart of the great metropolis, Tokyo. And to Charles and Lettie, the strange new world of rickshas, kimonos, chopsticks, paper windows, and the melodic clop of wooden shoes was sometimes quaint, sometimes fantastic, often bewildering.

Their first home consisted of two upstairs rooms behind the Bible school classrooms in downtown Tokyo. Their bed—a mattress stuffed with bamboo leaves. A secondhand Japanese cookstove indicated which corner of the home served as the kitchen. Meals were prepared in odd-shaped Japanese utensils and served on dainty Japanese dishes. In a land and culture bewilderingly different and alive with a strange commingling of foreign sounds, Lettie presided over the little household with dignity, grace, and a robust good humor. The remarkable flexibility that would not desert her through a lifelong kaleidoscope of experiences was already evident. Apart from occasional remarks and sketchy glimpses, however, we are left to imagine the personal sacrifices that must have gone into the Cowmans' early years in Japan. On one occasion, we know, the only food in the house was a piece of bread and some tea, which they served without apology to their guest—a distinguished British author.

The infant work of the OMS, enjoying a rapid growth, demanded the constant care and attention of the Cowmans and Kilbournes. There was the responsibility for the supervision of the churches and the administration of the Bible school. The work load meant that often they were kept busy till midnight, and usually the clatter of wooden shoes and noisy banging of the neighbors' shutters heralded the predawn start of another day. Mornings and afternoons were crowded with school and church activities, and night after night an unremitting campaign of evangelistic services was held in the gospel hall. Students and seekers often remained to pray far into the night hours.

It was an incredibly demanding life. Physically tired, they spent of themselves with abandon. An observer described them as working as "though possessed." Indeed, they were possessed—possessed with certain awareness of the urgency of the hour and the unprecedented ripeness of the field. History would later prove them right; for Japan, those were in reality golden years of opportunity. The sight of Japanese daily coming to Christ was a tonic to weary bodies and exhausted spirits. In it they found constant renewal. "This is the greatest work in the world," they exulted. "This is *the* work!"

Immersed as he was in the work, Charles found it difficult to keep contact with an ever-increasing host of friends and supporters whose sincere inquiries begged immediate and thoughtful response. In addition the faithful Telegraphers Band, there were numbers of churches following the infant Society with their prayers and gifts. Every mail brought letters of inquiry concerning the mission's policies and objectives. Who was to answer letters stacked in an ominous pile on Charles Cowman's desk?

It was with the thought of easing her husband's burden that Lettie took her pen to answer letters and write brief articles describing the work of the OMS in Japan. In doing so, a ministry was born. Some were quick to recognize her gift. Her words were well chosen and she wrote with direct and artless beauty, telling the story of God at work in human lives. Later, the entire Christian world would appreciate this woman, whose intimate acquaintance with good literature and instinctive knack with words had prepared her for the role of one of the great devotional writers of our time.

Soon the first OMS publication, *Electric Messages,* was born—a forerunner of *The Missionary Standard.* Thus named because the Society had sprung from the Telegraphers Band, *Electric Messages* was at first a simple 16-page paper. For half a century, Mrs. Charles Cowman contributed to the OMS publication, and readers on every continent hungrily perused its pages for her rich wisdom and creative Scriptural insights.

From the year 1901, when the Cowmans first arrived in Japan, until their forced return in 1917, their lives were crowded with continual activity. Those years witnessed the completion of the Every Creature Crusade in Japan and the laying of unshakable foundations on which a great church would rise. From Japan, the Cowmans had watched the planting of the Korean church. Deeply rooted, this church, nourished by the blood of martyrs and spurred by the fires of persecution, was to outstrip all others and become a foremost example of a modern New Testament church.

To promote the expanding work, the Cowmans made several trips to the homeland and Great Britain. On these tours, Mrs. Cowman's genius as a public speaker quickly became apparent. Disarmingly direct, winningly gracious, charmingly animated, she could take her audience with a word, a gesture. Quietly, without resorting to histrionic or masculine gesticulations, she could communicate the white-hot fervor of her soul and share the excitement and nobility of their calling. She employed her gifts without apology in the interests of a needy world.

Mrs. Cowman was at her best before large audiences. The greater the task, the less adequate she felt; hence the better the opportunity to prove her Lord, she reasoned. The thought gave her glowing poise. At many camp meetings, the Cowmans appeared in what was then fascinating and unique garb—Japanese kimonos. Behind them was a large map of the Orient on which were charted the triumphs of the Every Creature Crusades. As a result of this public ministry, the name of the small mission reached an ever-enlarging circle of friends —friends remarkable for their loyalty, and keystones in a worldwide constituency that would stand by the OMS through the long, difficult war years. Many of those loyalties were based on a personal acquaintance with Lettie Cowman and the impact of that single radiant life.

While still apparently strong and in his prime, Charles Cowman sensed he was nearing the end of his life's work. One evening he said to Lettie, ''I want to walk up the hill with you. I have a secret to tell you.''

That evening as the glow of a dying sun put a rim of gold over the mountains, he told her in a voice that sent a shaft of pain through her usually buoyant spirit, ''I have been having such heart pains at night,'' he said, ''I fear I will die. If I go on with the crusade, I will die. If I do not go on, there are millions who will die without hearing of Christ.''

The crusade would go on, but its general would be forced to retire from the conflict. Hopeful friends spoke of a short rest, recuperation, and then a return to the field. But for Charles Cowman, the fuel was all but spent. To the Cowmans, helplessness and inactivity seemed a fate worse than death. A once-strong man was reduced to weakness and utter dependence, to watch from the invalid's couch the progress of the crusade that had so long been his life. This was the exquisite agony that was the ultimate test of faith.

To understand the effect of Charles' suffering upon Lettie Cowman, one must understand the unusual relationship that existed between this husband and wife. Theirs was a devotion embodying at the same time the noblest of romantic ideals and the highest concepts of spiritual union. Years never diminished, but rather increased, the fervor of this devotion. Lettie's love for Charles can only be described as bordering on adoration. People remember that she always spoke his name with a certain awe, even reverence. She never ceased to cherish him as her hero. During her last interview she insisted, ''Give me no credit for writing *Streams*; there never would have been a *Streams* if it had not been for Charles Cowman. Give me no credit for the OMS; if it had not been for Charles Cowman there would be no

OMS. Give me no credit for World Gospel Crusades. Without Charles Cowman there would never have been a World Gospel Crusades.'' She never ceased to think of herself as primarily and essentially his helpmeet—a devoted wife perpetuating and carrying out her hero's divine vision.

Now, witness the scene. Charles Cowman is dying. His wife is also dying; she is dying another sort of death. It is the death that will bring her to that awful submission in which the object loved more than life itself is relinquished to His purposes. But this kind of death does not come easily. Her diary provides small windows into the drama being enacted. Amid terrifying doubts, they struggle for an answer. ''Three weeks and practically no sleep,'' she writes, ''. . . tonight the pain and agony, the living death. . . .'' Once, only once, is it written in her diary, ''This is a living hell on earth!''

More than relinquishing a life, it appeared that she must relinquish certain principles, once boldly asserted with a shining face and resounding certainty. What of healing? Does God not honor the prayer of faith and heal the sick? Had not scores of believing saints gone to their knees to plead for the life of Charles Cowman? What of those prayers? Through the furor of questions came a voice, ''Are you more intent on his healing than upon discovering the purposes of God?''

With a new desperation, she turned to those sources that had so often given succor in the past. The Word, long enjoyed, now became more than her necessary food. It stood as the final bulwark between her soul and blank despair. Hours were also spent haunting second-hand bookstores. Her practiced eye had learned to track down choice volumes, dusty and all but forgotten on some dingy shelf. Through the sleepless midnight hours, long after the city was silent, she sat drawing from the volumes draughts of courage. Hungrily she devoured the pages marking, noting, jotting down rare truths to fortify her soul. Little did she know that the solace she was finding was not for herself alone; that in God's larger purposes, she was amassing a fortune in consolation for generations of disconsolate ones. *Streams in the Desert* was being fashioned in the crucible of suffering. Later when a friend asked about the singular success of this book, she replied, ''The other books were written. *Streams* was born.''

The valley was six years long and ever darkening. After Charles' death she found a slip of paper in the Bible addressed to her. It was hard to decipher and the message might be even harder to carry out. ''Go on with the unfinished task,'' it read.

''The unfinished task.'' The words never seemed to be far from her consciousness. It was Charles' passion, a passion that even the last agonies of death had not corrupted. Now in the absence of her beloved's physical presence, she committed herself anew to the fulfillment of his vision. ''If I were to step into heaven today,'' she later said, ''Charles would ask, 'What are you doing here? Is the task finished?' ''

A short time later she dreamed that a familiar highway extended before her. She recognized it as a road where she and Charles had walked together in the bliss of childhood. But they came to a turn in the road. At this point, the Lord appeared to take Charles away, but doing so he turned to her. ''You will walk with Me along this shadowed pathway,'' He said. ''I will always be at your side. Charles' work on earth is finished. He has drunk the cup and been baptized into suffering. Now he is at home.'' To this Lettie responded, ''Thy will be done.''

But the vision, even the inspiration of Charles' life, could not dull the numbing sensation of aloneness that swept over her after his passing. In the place of the heaven-born union now seemed utter desolation. Her heart seemed dead. During this period, she seemed to have no sensible presence of the Lord. Alone, so alone. Alone in the house, alone in the quiet time, alone in the Word, alone in the bookshop, alone amidst friends, alone in the crowds. Sometimes a stifling sense of guilt seemed to settle down upon her. She felt that she was battling through what she should have been believing through. And what of the future? She was 53 years of age. What remained for the aging widow of a missionary executive?

Instead of falling into the trap of self-pity, however, she began to praise. Through the past six years she had uncovered a rare formula. ''My plan is to shun the spirit of sadness,'' she says in a *Streams* reading. ''I shun sadness as I would Satan himself.'' This she did by turning to praise. Her life became a continual exhortation to praise. Two classic devotional pieces (still being printed today) came from her pen at this time, *After All There is God* and *Praise Changes Things*. In the latter she explained, ''Many homes display the motto 'Prayer Changes

Things' and great blessing has resulted from this simple statement. We are all aware that prayer does change things. We know also, that many times the enemy has not been moved one inch from his stronghold although we have persisted in prayer for days and months—yes, and often years. Such was my own experience when passing through a time of great pressure and prayer did not change things. I came into possession of a wonderful secret. The secret is simply this: After we have prayed and believed, PRAISE CHANGES THINGS.''

In another place she testified, ''It was a dark night in my life when the words, 'Praise waiteth for Thee, O God in Zion,' were impressed upon my mind. I had been waiting in prayer for months. The months were now stretching into years—piled up as it were before God. Could not I now wait in praise before I saw the answer, or must I wait for signs and wonders ere I believed His Word? God was waiting for me to take this final step in faith, and when I began to praise Him for the answer, to wait in praise, to 'rest in the Lord and wait patiently for Him,' He began to answer in a manner that was exceedingly abundant above all that I could ask or think. The possession of that secret of victory has transformed my life and filled it with unutterable gladness.''

Awaiting the further unfolding of God's plan for her, Mrs. Cowman began arranging her collection of devotional pieces and writings. Some were sent to a religious journal, *God's Revivalist,* where her contributions appeared regularly for three years. Grateful readers requested that these devotional pieces be assembled in book form. Moreover, there came to her the growing conviction that God would have her pass on to others the comfort wherewith she herself had been comforted of God. Thus she began work on a book of devotional readings, one for every day of the year. God had already given her a title, taken from Isaiah 35:6. The volume would be called *Streams in the Desert.*

The publisher felt certain that the first edition of *Streams* would also be the last. Three thousand copies, he reasoned, would more than satisfy the demands of personal acquaintances and friends of the mission.

With that first small and unheralded edition by a hitherto unknown author, *Streams in the Desert* began one of the most phenomenally successful careers in the publishing business. Today the book remains one of the choicest of literary properties and the incessant demands from the public have called for more than fifty printings.

Readers were not slow in discovering that here was a devotional of more than ordinary worth. The insightful readings, sensitively arranged, ministered particularly to an always large group of God's people—those who were experiencing a "backside of the desert" period, as Mrs. Cowman termed it. These were people baffled by suffering, illness, disappointment, bereavement; those who felt that they were all but forgotten by God. *Streams* spoke to those who had difficulty relating their own sufferings to the noble and eternal purposes of a loving and all-wise God. The encouragement to unyielding faith that, despite all evidence to the contrary, sees God's loving purposes in all things is the repeated theme of this book. The message then today comes as a veritable stream of life in a wilderness of despair.

In explaining how *Streams* came to be, Mrs. Cowman wrote many years later, "In the year 1373, Julian of Norwich wrote, 'He said not, thou shalt not be tempted, thou shalt not be afflicted; but He did say, thou shalt not be overcome.' We are to rise unvanquished after every blow; we are to laugh the laugh of faith, not fear. To preserve the fruits of a triumph one must help his fellow-warriors to gain a similar conquest. The strong muscular limbs of a soldier are retained by sharing his blood with the entire army. For this cause, *Streams in the Desert* was born. Its lessons shared have resulted in a fellowship with many thousands over earth's domain."

After *Streams,* Mrs. Cowman felt certain that God would have her preserve in writing the vision of Charles Cowman. She must write his life story. The task loomed before her large and insurmountable. Still wondering how to begin, something written by the poetess Frances R. Havergal came as an encouragement: "Just in proportion to my sense of personal insufficiency in writing anything, God sends His blessing and power with it...I can't, but really I can't write a single verse unless I go to Him for it and get it from Him."

A comfortable home far from distractions was made available to Mrs. Cowman, and there she settled down to complete the task. From poignant recollections still vivid in her consciousness, she set forth the image of her hero. The result was *Charles Cowman: Missionary-Warrior.* If the story suffers from lack of objectivity and an over-idealism, and if a halo is too often visible, the book is not lacking for want of challenge. Burdened with sentiment as it is, the biography is, nevertheless, a book of fire. As one has said, "It was her dramatic flinging of Charles Cowman's burning torch to others." And many a young person after reading *Missionary-Warrior* resolved by the grace of God to take up that torch. Years later, when informed that the book was temporarily out of print, a missionary exclaimed, "That's a tragedy. There's no book I know quite like *Missionary-Warrior.* I'll never get over the impression it left upon my life."

One Thursday morning in March, 1931, Mrs. Cowman was called to the phone, never realizing that the call would eventuate in yet another devotional book. At the other end was a broken-hearted parent. Tearfully he explained that their only child, a two-and-a-half-year-old daughter, had been suddenly taken from them in an auto accident. "Do you think you could come over?" he pleaded.

Looking into the faces of two parents masked with horror of an unbearable grief, Mrs. Cowman seemed to see them as representatives of many who amid the shock of a sudden bereavement are reaching for some straw of consolation. She determined that for these parents she would daily gather poems, quotations, insights into the Word— offerings of consolation. Many of these pieces would later appear in a second devotional appropriately described by the very word *Consolation.*

The bereaved and disappointed seemed immediately to sense that in Mrs. Cowman they had a tender ally, a friend who would take their burdens to the throne making them her own. During World War II, the son of a well-known mission executive served on a United States destroyer which was sunk by enemy bombs. It was almost certain that the young man had perished. The father asked Mrs. Cowman to pray. Later he found her radiantly happy, rejoicing in God's deliverance. "Not a bone of him is broken," she declared. "God told me so. He gave me the assurance from His Word." Every report, however, indicated that the son had been lost in action. In time, however, a message came from the son stating that he had been blown off the deck into the ocean by the force of the explosion. Though severely bruised, not a bone had been broken.

On another occasion, the head of a large publishing house came to Mrs. Cowman during one of her frequent visits to the Moody Bible Institute. Desperately he explained that his business was on the rocks and there seemed to be no way of saving it. "Do pray for me," he requested earnestly. Later when they met again Mrs. Cowman reported, "Seven times I tried to pray for you, but all I can do is praise the Lord. I know He is going to do wonderful things for you." Her assurance was to prove well founded. Business began to improve, and today the gentleman is owner of a prospering international Christian publishing house.

During this period, Mrs. Cowman was preparing yet another manuscript. This third devotional book would bear the title *Springs in the Valley* and would be a companion volume to *Streams in the Desert.* The reception accorded *Streams,* along with the public's enthusiastic response to her regular contributions to religious magazines, had established Mrs. Cowman as a Christian author of considerable stature. Yet she would protest, "I am not an author. I am a missionary. I never set about to write a book. Only when God gives me messages to strengthen my fellow warriors do I preserve these messages in written form." On one occasion she was heard to say, "I do not find materials; materials come to me, fly to me from all over the world." These materials she found in an unlikely tract; an old, faded booklet; a crumpled church bulletin; or a tattered song book. While at work on *Springs in the Valley,* she recalled seeing a verse entitled, "Leave the Miracle to Him." She was convinced that the verse contained a message God would have her include in her book. But how to locate the piece? Why not ask the Father to send it, she reasoned. Several days later, a paper came from England. There it was—"Leave the Miracle to Him."

Following the death of Charles Cowman, his capable colleague and closest friend, E. A. Kilbourne, took the helm of the growing missionary organization. Only four years later, however, his earthly term of service expired and The Oriental Missionary Society was again without a president.

When Mrs. Cowman stepped into the role of missionary executive, there were questions in the minds of many. A devotional writer? Yes. An inspirational speaker, missionary, woman of faith? Certainly. But what did the aging widow, now approaching sixty, know of the complicated world of finance; the infinite and tedious details of bookkeeping, passports, visas, international regulations; the handling of properties, deeds, building contracts? Some regarded the step as hopelessly naive. Mrs. Cowman simply saw in it another adventure of faith; one more opportunity to put God to the test. And so with characteristic optimism, she set up headquarters at 900 North Hobart Boulevard, gathering her dedicated staff about her to daily communicate to them the ardor of her own spirit. Above her desk she placed a motto. The inscription summed up her outlook for the future: "God is able to give thee much more than this."

It was this same emphasis that a young missionary en route to India, Wesley Duewel, would later remember. "Mrs. Cowman," he said, "was almost Pauline in her approach to things. When we were in her home just before sailing for India, she gave us the Scripture verse, 'I will do better things for you than at your beginnings.' She was not just on the defensive. She was always ready to take the initiative for God."

In 1933 at the age of sixty-three, Mrs. Cowman decided that God would have her visit the work in China. At that time, Japan had invaded Manchuria and her armies were fanning out across the mainland in waves of destruction and terror. After observing the progress of the work in Peking and encouraging the missionaries, Mrs. Cowman went south to the Shanghai center and from there to Seoul, Korea. In Seoul, missionaries from the three fields of Japan, Korea, and China had gathered at the Bible school for a spiritual retreat.

Those were unforgettable days. Seething political and national turbulence was stirring all of Asia. None knew when hostilities would erupt into a violent and calamitous war. Amid the perplexity of the times, Mrs. Cowman gathered the missionaries around the Word to trace again the ageless promises of "things that cannot be shaken." In answer to the inevitable question, "What will become of the work?" came to her a growing certainty. "Missionaries may leave," she asserted, "but the work will go on because it has been built on nationals and the gates of hell shall not prevail against it." This had been the unshakable conviction of Charles Cowman. At this time she wrote a friend, "Native evangelism was born from above to meet the drastic challenge at a crucial hour." The heroic record of national Christians facing indescribable tortures and persecution would prove how correct she was.

Although Mrs. Cowman felt her heart drawn strongly toward Asia, she received a certain and inescapable impression that God did not want her to remain on the field. Even missionaries had insisted,

"Mrs. Cowman, you fight for us in another way, in another place. You can better care for us somewhere else."

One night she opened the Word to II Samuel 21 and "Thou shalt go no more out with us to battle. . . it is better that thou succor us out of the city." Within a month, she was on board ship bound once more for the United States.

She arrived home in Los Angeles exhausted, her strength spent. After a physical examination a physician announced, "Your heart is too weak to stand the strain. I advise you to immediately discontinue all public ministry. To disobey may be to drop dead." These words were almost identical to the ones a doctor had used in so accurately describing the condition of Charles Cowman, followed by the same stern words of warning. Did this for her also signal the end of an active public ministry and the commencement of a gradual and painful retirement? She could not accept it as such. A scrap of poem she stumbled across seemed to be God's message to her:

> This hour a grander work awaits your hand
> Than any written in the treasured past.
> Lay to the oar! The tide runs fast,
> Life's possibilities are yet unspanned.

And from her worn Bible came the assurance, "Thou shalt prolong the King's life."

When an invitation came to speak at the Little Country Church of Hollywood, Mrs. Cowman believed that God would have her accept, and she put it, "Let Him do what seemeth best." Her faithful nurse and companion, Lydia Bemmels, stationed herself on the platform, hypodermic needle ready for any emergency.

As Mrs. Cowman spoke, she became aware that something unusual was taking place in her body. Fatigue was replaced with rest; weakness vanished as she sensed a flow of abundant strength. Instantly, it seemed, healing was hers. A subsequent physical check revealed that her heart was absolutely normal. Ten years later she would still be addressing large rallies with the same fervor and crowds would marvel at her youthful animation, her seemingly inexhaustible enthusiasm.

In 1936 the arrival of a cable from Swansea, Wales, touched off a chain of circumstances which was to literally fulfill the promise contained in the snatch of poetry: ". . .a grander work awaits your hand than any written in the treasured past.''

The cable invited Mrs. Cowman to speak at an ''Every Creature Convention'' to be held at the Swansea Bible Institute in Wales. She knew the school well and remembered that it was a monument to the incredible faith and prayer life of Reese Howells. (His life is dramatized in the book *Reese Howells Intercessor.*)

At the Bible college, Mrs. Cowman found that a host of missionaries from many lands had gathered. After her first message, Reese Howells came to her to say, ''We want you to speak every night of the conference.''

As she told of Charles' vision and the triumphs of the Every Creature Crusade, the vision like a divine incendiary was igniting one heart after another. Those present recalled that the atmosphere was charged with heavenly activity. Growing illumination left listeners more than inspired—some came away with a clear-cut plan of action to carry out the ''Every Creature'' plan in their field.

Following the convention, Reese Howells, whose life is a continuous illustration of divine guidance, spoke to Mrs. Cowman. ''Remain in your room,'' he insisted. ''We will send meals to you. God has something to tell you.''

At 6:00 a.m. Monday morning, August 10, 1936, the message came, ''I have sanctified thee and ordained thee a prophet unto the nations.'' What was God trying to tell her? ''A prophet to the nations.'' To the nations? What more could she, a widow past sixty, do as a ''prophet to the nations''? Perhaps she was a victim of delusions, a common phenomenon among the aging who look back with fond recollection upon more active days.

But the conviction remained inescapable. Gradually the plan took shape before her, bold and exciting. She was to carry out Charles' Every Creater Crusade vision. She has to be God's instrument in planting the gospel in millions of homes in many nations. Quietly she recalled Charles' final words, ''Go on with the unfinished task.''

On Sunday of the following week as she walked across the lawn of the beautiful Bible school garden, she met Anna Liisa and Sanfrid Mattsson, who had just arrived from Finland. The Swansea Every Creature Conference and the report of the crusades in Japan had fired them with a vision for Finland.

Three hours of conversation with the Mattssons left Mrs. Cowman numb with a consciousness of God's presence. She had heard more than the pleadings of two of God's children, she had heard the divine command. She must accompany the Mattssons to Finland.

Mrs. Cowman had not come to Wales with any notion of extending the trip northward to Finland. God would have to provide funds, clothing, ship passage. Countless details would have to be worked out. Soon, however, it became clear to all the plan was more than a human whim. Every need was supplied. Funds arrived. A fur coat was loaned her for the Northland. The captain of the freighter on which the Mattssons were booked even released his own cabin so that she might accompany them to Finland.

When the *Kadir,* a Finnish lumber ship, left Cardiff, Wales, the voyage promised nothing unusual. Before long, however, a mounting wind was driving the ocean into mountains of waves that rose and fell with increasing force. Several days later, passengers noted an ominous sign. The sky had darkened, and the water had turned from a rich blue to a deep, inky green. Cargo was lashed down and furniture secured; the passengers were ordered below. A violent gale now whipped the waves into a ferocious world of water that threatened at any moment to annihilate the staggering vessel. A radio confirmed the ferocity of the storm. "Some ships," it reported, "have floundered and sunk; others have been carried against the northern cliffs and dashed to pieces." Some, still afloat, frantically sent SOS signals as they were driven towards dangerous rocks and reefs.

The *Kadir's* cook, a hardy Estonian woman, made her way through the heaving ship to find a passenger whose majestic imperturbability seemed to be the only calm on the whole trembling ocean. "This is terrible, terrible," she moaned. "We've never had a sea like this. We are in awful danger! The ship cannot stay much longer."

Tenderly Mrs. Cowman embraced the terrified woman urging her to trust in the Lord Jesus as her Saviour, and commending them both with all on board to His mercy. Surely "the vision" was not to end with a doomed ship and murky coffin at the bottom of the North Sea!

To halt the vessel's plunging course toward the deadly reefs, the captain ordered that the anchor be lowered. For two days and nights they were flung helplessly about, entirely at the mercy of the frenzied waves.

Then it was over. A brilliant sun dispersed the leaden sky and shone down upon a quieted ocean. Arriving at port in Finland, they descended a swaying rope ladder onto the remains of a luckless wharf that had been largely demolished by the storm. Their voyage had been extended 14 days. But they were in Finland. This was the beginning of the fulfillment of Mrs. Cowman's call to the nations. Crusades launched during the following months were to cover large segments of Europe and several countries soon to be stranded behind Communism's grim Iron Curtain.

At Jackobstadt, they were greeted by Christians who had been in prayer for six days in preparation for their arrival. The next evening a missionary meeting was held. To the waiting crowd, Mrs. Cowman recounted the call of Charles Cowman, his vision to take the gospel to "every creature," and the dramatic fulfillment of that vision in Japan. The narrative that had so often fired the imaginations of listeners again seemed stirringly relevant. Her message concluded with a bold plan of action. Then she called for volunteers. Young men quickly stepped out in response to the challenge.

The following day crusade leaders pored over a map of Finland, charting the course the crusade would take. First, Finland would be covered with Scriptures in a systematic house-to-house campaign. Detailed maps of every area would be obtained and every advance recorded. Next, the crusaders would carry large packs of Scriptures to Lapland. They were to travel by sled or skis over snow-swept mountains and to remote ice-locked villages. Finally it was determined that Estonia's two million were also to get the Word.

Once the battle plan had been formulated, they calculated the financial cost of the effort. The entire venture would take not less than $10,000.00—a sum of money that no one had. No one but God. At this point, Mrs. Cowman quoted a familiar and oft-proven principle: "God's man in God's place at God's work done in God's way will never lack God's support," she assured them.

While evangelist-crusaders, laden with Gospels, began their systematic coverage of Finland, Mrs. Cowman journeyed into the distant areas of Lapland. Protected from the winter blasts by fur coat and woolen leggings, she climbed aboard a picturesque reindeer sleigh to be drawn over the frozen expanses. Small school houses were filled to capacity with scores who had come great distances to hear a unique woman tell about the power of God's Word.

Meanwhile in Finland, crusaders found that the Scriptures prayerfully and systematically placed in each home were like torches touched to dry kindling. And whole towns, long anesthetized by the sterile formalism of a state religion, found themselves infected by the spiritual contagion of these evangelists. When Mrs. Cowman returned to the Finnish capital, a union crusade rally was arranged in the parliament building. Leading citizens and political figures were present. "When Christ said that the gospel was to go to every creature," she explained without apology, "He meant nothing other than to every creature."

Everywhere the crusade was leaving in its wake fires of revival. Many witnessed that this renewed emphasis upon the divine Word was having a noticeable effect upon entire communities and churches. Young people were stirred by the sight of other young people in action. One youth, a gifted Finnish pianist, testified that God had called him to work among the Jews. Another reported a call to China. And many laymen—grass roots evangelists—moved out with urgency to proclaim Christ.

From Finland the crusade moved to Estonia where it also reached eighty thousand Russian refugees from Communism. From there it spread to Latvia, Poland, Czechoslovakia.

Back in London, Mrs. Cowman met with Bible societies making bold demands and calling for massive orders of Scriptures. Now, even in the British Isles, concerned Christians were being jolted by the possibilities of Every Creature Crusades. Leaders in Scotland confessed, "We are simply stunned over this thing. To think that God had to send you clear from China to Los Angeles and then here to arouse us to action." A Baltic States Committee was formed. What had happened in Finland, Estonia, and Japan must also take place in other countries.

The Every Creature Crusades in Europe marked the last significant evangelical thrust in some ill-fated countries soon to be crushed by the senseless tyranny of Naziism or to fall prey to the greedy paw of Communism.

Using Great Britain as a home base, Mrs. Cowman spent the following months in missionary journeys that took her to Switzerland, Paris, Luxembourg, and the Middle East. Everywhere she found *Streams* readers, and at every opportunity she sought to communicate the crusade vision. These travels brought her in contact with a host of stimulating and influential persons. In Zurich, Switzerland, she was guest of a noble family that opened their home for drawing room meetings. In Alexandria, she was granted a private interview with an 18-year-old youth soon to be crowned king. His name was Prince Farouk. She witnessed to him clearly, presenting him with a copy of the gospels especially bound in royal blue.

In Jerusalem, a visit to a factory where exquisite china is fired provided her with an object lesson she would use all over the world. In one corner she noted some beautiful china apparently discarded.

"Why is it there?" she asked.

"Oh, it was to be a chandelier in the king's palace," came the reply, "but it would not take the fire."

"It would not take the fire," she repeated to herself, seizing upon the words and seeing in them an intensely meaningful spiritual application. She asked for a piece of the discarded china. She would show it to many an audience challenging them, "No matter how hot God's furnace, take the fire!"

Back in England she was invited to be the guest of His Imperial Majesty Haile Selassie, exiled king of Ethiopia. His land had been wrested from him by the ruthless armies of Mussolini. The dictator had boasted that he would make the tiny country part of The New Roman Empire.

In the presence of the Emperor, Mrs. Cowman opened the Scriptures to Isaiah 54 and read, "For a small moment I have forsaken thee; but with great mercies will I gather thee. In a little wrath I hid my face from thee for a moment; but with everlasting kindness will I have mercy on thee, saith the Lord thy Redeemer." This, she boldly assured the Emperor, meant that his exile was but for a brief time. The ruthless Mussolini would shortly be vanquished by the wrath of the Almighty.

In appreciation for the visit, the Emperor presented Mrs. Cowman with a ring of heavy Abyssinian gold known as the gold of Ophir. Then he remarked, "Since I have been in England, you are the only person who has ever spoken to me in this way about the Lord Jesus Christ. We deeply appreciate it." The scene marked the establishment of a lifelong friendship—one that Emperor Haile Selassie would honor years later when, once more restored to his country, he would make a celebrated tour of the United States.

In the year 1941, Mrs. Cowman at 71 was impressed that she must attend the World Sunday School Convention in Mexico City. Seven hundred delegates from every republic in Latin America were to be present.

"Why has God brought me here?" she asked herself upon her arrival at the convention. She might easily and more logically have sent Dr. Serrano, the Spanish translator of *Streams*. Yet she remained confident that she was there on a divine errand, to keep God's appointment.

Following the convention, a large Methodist church in Mexico City invited her to speak. Noted missionary author, Dr. Heugel, was her interpreter. After the message, a young lady approached Mrs. Cowman. In her outstretched hand she held a peso (about 20 cents).

"This is to begin a crusade in Mexico," she said with childlike simplicity.

A peso. What was a peso among the millions of Mexico? Quickly the Holy Spirit rebuked her, saying, "Give ye them to eat." A peso —plus God. Millions in Mexico could be fed.

A second invitation came. This time she was asked to address the student body at the Union Seminary in Mexico City. That morning 60 students heard the challenge to take up the crusade torch. Listening to Mrs. Cowman was also Captain Alexandro Guzman, Mexico's dynamic Salvation Army leader. As a Catholic youth, he had been saved through the secret reading of a Scripture portion. Captain Guzman came away from the service strangely burdened.

On the morning of July 29, 1941, the hotel desk informed Mrs. Cowman that there was a telephone call for her. Dr. Frederick Heugel and Captain Guzman were on the line.

"Captain Guzman and I must see you immediately," said Dr. Heugel.

"Certainly, where can we meet?"

"In the seminary prayer room."

"Good, I'll be there."

As Dr. Heugel entered the small sanctuary, it was with the announcement, "Captain Guzman and I spent last night in prayer. Mrs. Cowman, God has given us a vision for a gospel crusade for all Mexico."

"Do you know what a crusade costs?" was Mrs. Cowman's instant reply. "It cost the life of my husband. You should not begin unless you are ready to go to the death."

"We have counted the cost and are ready," the men answered.

"Do you know what such a crusade costs in money?" she went on. "It costs thousands of dollars. I have only a widow's two empty hands, but I promise I will give you whatever God puts in them."

In the stillness of the prayer room, Mrs. Cowman understood why God had brought her to Mexico. Suddenly her heart filled with unspeakable joy. Before leaving Mexico, she placed an order with the Bible Society for the first 100,000 Gospels. The bill arrived in Los Angeles before she did, a bill for $878.05.

In the office the following Monday, Mrs. Cowman handed the treasurer, Frances Black, a contribution of $15.00 asking her to total the gifts that had been received for the Mexico Crusade.

The office staff was called together for a prayer meeting. But curiously, the service was turned into a time of praise. Soon Frances returned with the report. "The amount we presently have on hand for the Mexico Crusade," she announced, "is exactly $878.05."

On December 1, 1941, seven days before Pearl Harbor, the Mexico Crusade officially began. (In Mexico it was called the National Evangelistic Campaign.) Soon the reports were arriving: "Seven thousand homes visited... greater sale of the Bible and Bible portions than ever before." When Dr. Guzman held a week's services in one large church, 200 members responded to the call for crusade volunteers. The fire continued to spread as the 110 churches of the Mexico Presbyterian Synod committed themselves to the effort.

Dr. Heugel reported, "God is blessing the crusade beyond anything we had dreamed. I never saw a church so moved. Churches are calling the crusade leaders faster than they can respond. The crusade is looming up as the greatest thing on Mexico's missionary horizon."

Later he wrote, "People are saying this is the greatest evangelistic work ever seen in Mexico."

And finally, "A tidal wave of revival is sweeping over Mexico. The nation is being stirred as never before. Like a mighty stream the National Evangelistic Crusade, launched December 1, 1941, is sweeping everything before it."

Dismayed, the Roman Catholic Church launched their own Gospel distribution program—something hitherto unheard of in Mexico.

"Wonderful," exulted Captain Guzman, "after all, you can't put out fire with gasoline."

As the crusade continued its onslaught, enemy forces resorted to violence in an effort to check the progress of the evangelicals. Local priests ordered their zealots to drive the crusaders out. One crusader was martyred, ten others wounded. In one village, two crusaders retreated when they came upon a couple of battered bodies, gruesome evidence of the violent disposition of the townspeople. Checked by the Holy Spirit, however, they returned to the village resolved to fulfill the purpose for which they had come. "You start distributing on this side of town," the captain directed, "and I'll begin on the other side. We'll meet in the market place, or we'll meet in heaven."

Final statistics of the Mexico Crusade read, "Participants: 11 denominations, 180 congregations, 180 ministers, 30 prominent laymen, 1,500 workers. Number of gospels distributed: 1,455,000."

"I had not had such guidance in more than forty years," Mrs. Cowman wrote of an experience that was to completely reshape The Oriental Missionary Society. "I had retired to a quiet room in a small hotel in Winona Lake, Indiana, presumably to work on a book. But I could not write. I spent three days in an agony of soul burden. What could it mean?" Her attention was drawn inexplicably to Judges 1:15 and the words, "Thou has given me a southland."

The year was 1942. War had closed doors to Europe. In Asia, the work of The Oriental Missionary Society had been forced to a virtual standstill. Missionaries in China had been herded into huge concentration camps.

"Thou has given me a southland." Could this mean that the OMS was to enter the field of Latin America? There was no escaping it. The impression refused to leave.

The Cowmans had never seriously envisaged work in South America. The very name of the society seemed to preclude anything of this sort. Now, what of this strong inner urge? The voice, she recognized. She knew well that she dare not ignore it.

"All right, Lord," she finally conceded, "Latin America, then, it must be. But You must send us a man to lead the advance into the field." For days she waited before the Lord with this single petition, "Lord, send us Your man."

The plea was still in her heart some time later when on a tour of the

Free Methodist Publishing House she met Dr. Ben Pearson, editor of their youth publication. Dr. Pearson had not only served as a general superintendent of the denomination's youth organization, he was also a veteran of twenty years' service as superintendent of Mexican Missions in the Southwest. These facts registered very quickly in Mrs. Cowman's mind. More than this, here was a man whose reckless faith and huge love for people distinguished him as a leader shaped from the same mold as Mrs. Cowman herself. Both immediately sensed a warm kinship—that rare meeting of minds and spirits committed to and mastered by a common purpose. Before leaving, Mrs. Cowman felt led to say, "Pray for me, Dr. Pearson, I have a call to South America."

Dr. Pearson could not shake off the effect of that brief meeting. Several months later, two application forms appeared on Mrs. Cowman's desk. At the bottom were signatures that made her heart suddenly leap: "Ben and Emma Pearson."

"Have you a call from God, Dr. Pearson?" was Mrs. Cowman's first question when she reached him by phone.

"I have," was the immediate reply. Mrs. Cowman had found God's man.

In August, 1943, Dr. Pearson and William Gillam were sent to establish a beachhead in Colombia, South America. Soon after they arrived they were joined by John Palmer, an English missionary who had served for a number of years in Latin America. Missionary directors Harry Woods and Edwin Kilbourne arrived later to help locate a suitable property where a Bible training center could be built. They found a beautiful estate, *Les Cerezes* (The Cherry Trees), just outside the city of Medellin. The owner, for health reasons, was being forced to sell the property. He was asking $20,000.00, a large sum, but actually only about half what the property was worth. Dr. Pearson, William Gillam, and the visiting directors were satisfied that this was God's chosen site for the OMS work in Colombia. In a step of faith, they fixed their signatures to the contract, committing the OMS to the purchase of *Les Cerezes*.

"Frances, God wants us to empty the *Streams in the Desert* treasury and send it to South America. Our brethren there are needing money." The directive came without warning one morning as Miss Frances Black busied herself with the accounts. Frances had learned to respect Mrs. Cowman's sudden impulses, yet she hesitated. Could it be that today she was acting hastily? After all, there was $20,000.00 in the fund. No word had been received from the directors in South America requesting funds.

Soon enough, however, she discovered that in Mrs. Cowman's mind the matter was an urgent one and there was no delaying the issue. "Frances, have you forwarded the *Streams* money?" Mrs. Cowman asked later that same day. This time Frances was not slow to comply with the unusual request. Later it was surprising only to those who knew little of the ways of God and the faith of Mrs. Cowman to learn that Dr. Pearson, Bill Gillam, and the OMS directors on the morning after they had signed the contract for "Les Cerezes" had an airmail envelope placed in their hands. The enclosed letter read: "God spoke to me. He said 'Empty the *Streams* treasury and send it to Colombia.' I do not know what this money is to be used for. I am sure He will make it clear to you when it arrives." Accompanying the letter were four checks for $5,000.00 each—exactly the amount needed.

In her seventy-fifth year, Mrs. Cowman made her final missionary journey to attend the dedicatory service of the new Bible seminary in Colombia and to witness the miracle that had its strange beginning that day in her Winona Lake hotel room.

On the field, she again recounted the leadings of her Lord; the mysterious providences that had moved her from Asia to Europe and then to Mexico and Latin America, striving to finish Charles Cowman's "unfinished task." Missionaries and nationals alike listened with quiet reverence. Primitive jungle Indians, often shy of the foreigners, were drawn irresistibly by the magnet of this beautiful soul that seemed to exude the love of God. They had no words to explain it. They simply understood here as in Japan, Korea, and Estonia: "The woman loves us." When the time came to leave, missionaries and nationals gathered at the airport in a memorable farewell scene.

As her plane circled and then disappeared over the rim of the Andes, it signaled the end of an era. A creative missionary of world stature had made her last journey to a foreign land.

Though a lifetime of foreign service had ended, it would be a mistake to suppose that for the remaining years of Mrs. Cowman's life she contented herself with the seclusion of a comfortable, well-earned retirement. The life that had given so unsparingly could not but continue to spontaneously spend itself for others until the last ounce of strength was exhausted. Following the example of the seasons, Mrs. Cowman was actually entering a glorious and colorful autumn of life —a period remarkable for its continuing creativity. Her pen, always busy, was still providing her publisher with manuscripts.

One morning a youth leader entered Mrs. Cowman's office with a strange request. "Give us a book for the youth of our generation," he said. Mrs. Cowman recalled the words of David, "When I am old and greyheaded, O God, forsake me not; until I have shewed thy strength unto this generation." In answer to the request came a classic devotional for young people entitled *Mountain Trailways for Youth.*

Following *Mountain Trailways* came yet another devotional volume; this one with a special ministry to the elderly was called *Traveling Toward Sunrise.* "Letters poured in to me from many in the eventide of life," Mrs. Cowman explained. "They felt caught in the web of discouragement—others felt unwanted. To this vast company, *Traveling Toward Sunrise* presents a reminder of God's unfailing promise, 'Even to your old age I am [your God]; I have made, and I will bear; even I will carry...you.' "

These two devotionals written in her seventies reveal the astonishing breadth of one woman's sensitivities. Concurrently she was able to minister words of understanding to youth while at the same time speaking to her own contemporaries as she accompanied them into the sunset years.

During these years Mrs. Cowman's ever-broadening vision conceived of two additional organizations. The services of publishing and gospel distribution, she concluded, could better be carried out by independent organizations not bound within the structure of The Oriental Missionary Society. This conviction led to the establishment of World Gospel Crusades and Cowman Publications.

Mrs. Cowman's resignation was accepted and she was given the deed to 256 South Hobart Boulevard, the small home where she and Charles had shared their Gethsemane and where *Streams* had been born.

On March 3, 1950, her eightieth birthday, Mrs. Cowman planned a reception to be held in the newly-remodeled home. As guests arrived, she presented each with a delightful booklet which she had written especially for the occasion. Its title: *Life Begins at Eighty.*

The small bungalow appropriately named "Oasis" was in fact all that its name implied. Its atmosphere was noticeably pregnant with divine presence. Now a world-renowned figure with books appearing in many languages, her guests included leaders from every walk of life who made pilgrimages to see her, to share with her their burden, to receive her benediction. Haile Selassie, on a tour of the U.S., made a special point to seek out his old friend at the Oasis to express again his appreciation for her prayers and encouragement through the dark days of World War II. Departing missionaries sought her out, all the while looking into her winsome features as though trying to discover for themselves the secret of this life.

Although still in demand as a speaker, failing eyesight now made public appearances increasingly painful. When a TV program requested that she appear before the cameras insisting that thousands of viewers were anxious to see her, she replied not ungraciously, "If people want to see me, let them read *Streams.* My picture is in *Streams.*"

These were years given to correspondence. Her still-glowing pen supplied touches of heaven to scores of fainting hearts. This ministry recognized no doctrinal or denominational distinctions. To each she gave some part of her spirit.

Meanwhile she kept daily contact with World Gospel Crusades and Cowman Publications, the two organizations which, with the OMS, sought to perpetuate the Cowman vision. Those who visited her home were treated to fresh reports of God at work. "Twenty thousand New Testaments in modern Greek have just gone to be distributed to the Greek army," she would exclaim excitedly, or, "Rejoice with me, the first half-million Gospels have just gone to Formosa in response to an appeal by Madame Chiang Kai-shek on behalf of the Nationalist soldiers."

"God tells me I will enter darkness in 1957. I do not know whether it is death or just a tunnel. When we have the light, we trust the light. When it is dark, we trust Him." Such was the announcement Mrs. Cowman made to the board of directors of Cowman Publications at her home on December 31, 1956. The message was delivered quietly, without self-pity or noticeable emotion. But there was an absolute finality about the pronouncement. None dared question her further.

"Enter darkness. " The directors wondered, could it mean blindness? For more than a decade she had been suffering from poor eyesight, and as early as 1940 had confided to a friend, "Pray for me. I fear I may lose my eyesight. " An operation to remove cataracts had been only partially successful. They knew that most of her reading now was done by listening to the voice of her faithful companion, Lydia Bemmels, as she read from some chosen volume.

It happened as Mrs. Cowman had said. In January, 1957, in her eighty-seventh year she entered a final dark corridor of her mortal life -three years of almost total disability from which she would never recover. Almost completely helpless, it was no longer possible for Miss Bemmels to care for her. Reluctantly, friends arranged to situate her in a rest home where she would receive the benefit of constant professional care.

Immediately following the move, she made lists of friends she wished to have come for a "farewell visit." She also listed the few cherished possessions she wanted given to friends. Whatever their intrinsic value, they were priceless to those who received them. They remained mementos of a remarkable life and trophies of great adventures for God. Among them were: a Chinese carved table; her silver service; a silver cup from the Koreans who later perished at the hands of Communists ("This," she explained, "must be used as a chalice."); a painting of her as a girl, face framed with gold locks; their marriage certificate; a bronze table bell; Oriental vases; a light gold chain worn when she was a child; a gold thimble; her Bibles, limp and crowded with markings from Genesis to Revelation; Charles' books and her library; and finally, Haile Selassie's covenant ring of the gold of Ophir.

When friends arrived for a last visit, she was too weak to stand. Yet with another helping her, she rose to deliver a final benediction in a scene reminiscent of Moses charging his people before his final solitary ascent of Mt. Nebo.

This was no time for small talk, for trite expressions of sympathy, or hollow words of cheer. God had told her that her time was approaching. She was certain about that. To friends who had so recently seen her talking youthfully in defiance of her years, the solemnity of that scene left them with a sense of sadness. Now, it seemed certain, she was leaving them. They departed feeling almost as if they were returning from a fresh grave.

After that she asked that no visitors see her—a request that many found difficult to understand. Now completely spent, it was as though the toll of years had finally caught up with her, subduing the flesh with devastating force. "I want my friends to remember me as I was," was all she would say. Flowers sent to her would quickly be forwarded to another room. From her, nurses would occasionally bring a report that recalled the old spirit: "The crusade must go on."

One night heaven's doors seemed to be opening. "Yes, Charles, I'm coming," she said and then, "Don't you see Jesus?" But days became months, and months years while concerned friends prayed and wondered how long the weakened frame could hold the once-irrepressible spirit.

Mrs. Cowman's biographer, Dr. B. H. Pearson, suggests, "There is something mysterious in these days. She had ministered to suffering all her life. She had written a volume that in recent years probably was the companion of more aching hearts than any book but the Bible. It seemed that as His Son in the garden was given, so God the Father was not giving her the cup to drink."

Release for Mrs. Charles Cowman's spirit came as the sun was sinking on Easter Sunday, April 17, 1960. Among her papers was found the following poem written in her familiar hand:

> Finish thy work, the time is short.
> The sun is in the west
> The night is coming down,
> Till then, think not of rest.
> Rest? Finish thy work then rest.
> Till then, rest never.

Epilogue

Just before Charles Cowman passed away, too weak to speak, he scribbled a few words on a piece of paper and handed it to his wife. The message read, "Go on. Go on." These dying words of Charles Cowman sum up the continuing spirit of the mission to which he gave birth. Despite temporary setbacks, closing doors and Satanic opposition, OMS has continued to advance on all fronts, ever seeking to fulfill our Lord's commission to witness to the uttermost part of the earth. The following is but a brief summary of the progress in its various fields.

With the Japanese attack on Pearl Harbor and the consequent involvement of the U.S. in World War II, the future of OMS seemed in jeopardy. On that bleak December morning in 1941, foreign missionary endeavor came to an abrupt halt on all of our major fields. Japan was now "the enemy," her cities target for Allied bombs. Many of our pastors and national workers were seized and imprisoned. Some were tortured for their refusal to take part in the so-called shrine worship of the Emperor of Japan. In China, where most of the country was already in Japanese hands, missionaries were herded into vast internment camps. Only India, where the Society had just opened work, remained open. And even here missionary efforts were hampered by the effects of the global conflict upon ocean travel and the flow of supplies. By 1942, as Japan's armies advanced through Southeast Asia, it appeared only a matter of time before India too would fall victim to the Empire's ruthless war machine.

V-J Day, 1945, finally brought an end to the second great war of the century, beginning an era of unprecedented growth for OMS and indeed for all evangelical missions. New adversaries, however, began to appear posing a fresh threat to the advance of the Gospel. International Communism, to be joined by the more subtle forces of nationalism and materialism, threatened to overpower the church. Secularism and liberalism sought to destroy it from within. Nevertheless for the most part, the work of OMS has shown heartening growth. At the same time, new fields have been continually opened until as of this writing (1999) they number 18 with workers in 29 countries. So the church grows and the gates of hell cannot prevail against it.

Japan

During the war years, the Christian community in Japan suffered fearful persecution. Many pastors were imprisoned, tortured and some martyred. Their flocks were scattered. The government, in an effort to control and restrict the church, decreed that all Protestant bodies be merged into a single united body—known as the Kyodan.

Following the war, OMS pastors were confronted with a painful choice— either to remain within the comfortable structure of the United Church or leave to begin the arduous task of rebuilding the OMS Japan Holiness Church. Many chose to remain in the Kyodan—about 80 pastors in all. Others who had been influenced by Juji Nakada worked independently. The remainder elected to join with Reverend Kurumada in the reestablishment of the denomination originally founded by OMS.

Kurumada, a diminutive but dynamic and Spirit-filled leader, was a graduate of Taylor University in the U.S. During the war he had suffered for his refusal to be silent on the doctrine of Christ's second coming—a dogma particularly anathema to the empire-minded military dictatorship. As head of the post-war church, he appealed to the OMS Board of Directors to immediately send missionaries to Japan to assist in the rebuilding of the church and seminary.

Although U.S. air raids had left the OMS center in the heart of Tokyo a devastation, soon missionaries were joining nationals in the task of clearing the bomb-scarred site; in short order, a new church and seminary along with missionary and national residences began to rise. As land values soared in the 1960's, this campus was sold and the OMS center relocated on a commodious property in the Higashi Murayami district of the city.

The years immediately following the war were a heyday for evangelism in Japan. Throngs turned to Christ everywhere, and although some of this was superficial, much has remained. Seizing the opportunity, OMS opened the second Every Creature Crusade(ECC), calling for young Crusaders (Western college and seminary students) to join teams of Japanese nationals to plant churches and place Scriptures in every home in the nation.

Today the Japan Holiness Church continues to enjoy steady growth in the face of an insidious materialism, now so much a part of the culture of the country. JHC churches total 169 congregations with 18 preaching points and a baptized membership of more than 12,000. Tokyo Bible Seminary continues to train ministers, evangelists and Christian workers and presently has about 100 students.

Although church and seminary ministries are today largely in the hands of nationals, foreign missionaries have found an effective evangelistic tool in the teaching of conversational English in local churches. Others serve on the staff and faculty of the Christian Academy of Japan (CAJ), the country's foremost school for the education of missionary children.

Korea

Once called "The Land of the Morning Calm," Korea's recent history has made a mockery of this charming epithet. Degraded to a Japanese colony in 1910, Koreans never resigned themselves to this insult. Volatile and fiercely independent by nature, they ceaselessly planned revolts and devised means to express their contempt for their overlords.

With the U.S. at war with Japan, it followed that the Korean church, which owed its birth to American missionaries, should become immediately suspect, a prime target for persecution. In short order, all Christian churches were closed, their pastors imprisoned, tortured, even killed. With unabated zeal, however, Korean believers met in secret to worship and make intercession without ceasing. Spiritual seed was being sown which would in time break forth in sweeping revival and unprecedented church growth. But first would come an even greater ordeal.

World War II over, the Korean church was unknowingly on the threshold of one of the most intense periods of tribulation to which any church has ever been subjected. In 1950, without warning, a vast Red army from the north swept down across the 38th parallel in an orgy of death and destruction. Again, special targets were the Christians. They were mercilessly terrorized; their leaders rounded up for mass executions. Hardly a Christian family came through the war unscathed. When the bloody epoch was over, the toll of martyrs exceeded the number that died for their faith during the notorious Roman persecutions in the early centuries of the church.

During the Korean War, 179 OMS churches were bombed, the mission center destroyed and along with it the seminary buildings, as well as national and missionary housing. When the Communist forces were finally repulsed, they left behind a scene of horrific devastation. Cities lay in rubble, widows resorted to prostitution and orphans wandered the streets crying for food.

The church and missionary community were not slow to reach out in compassion to the bleeding nation. At the same time they realized that cities full of crushed and despairing people were ripe as never before for the Gospel of hope. During the decade of 1953-1963, the Korean church enjoyed greater growth than in the previous 80 years of its history.

Today the Korean Evangelical Holiness Church (KEHC), fruit of OMS pioneer work, numbers nearly 2,900 churches, with a membership over 600,000. Twenty-five Every Creature Crusade teams are continuously involved in church planting efforts. Seoul Theological Seminary, now officially a university as well, has a student body of more than 2,000. KEHC presently has some 30 missionaries serving in foreign countries.

China

The end of World War II, far from bringing relief to China, heralded the beginning of a new and more agonizing struggle. This time the foe was Communism. More correctly the war with Japan was a hiatus in an ongoing contest between Generalissimo Chiang Kai Shek and Mao Tse Tung for supremacy going back to the 1920's. Mao and his Communist insurgents escaped annihilation by trekking eastward across China's northern provinces in the historic Long March. During the conflict with the Japanese, they regrouped, prepared and plotted the overthrow of the

Nationalist regime. Even before the departure of the defeated Japanese, the wheels of Mao's revolution were again in motion.

In the United States where war-weary Americans were understandably reluctant to involve themselves in another Asian conflict, apathy eventually gave way to concern and then, too late, to alarm as the objectives of international Communism became all too apparent. By 1949 the China mainland was in Mao's grasp; the remnants of the Nationalist government and army were in uneasy exile on the small island province of Taiwan, then known in the West as Formosa.

OMS leaders had watched with mounting anxiety the forced retreat of missionaries from China. First the Peking Bible Seminary was closed. Then as Communist troops pushed southward, mission centers in Shanghai, Nanking and finally Canton also fell into enemy hands. After a brief "honeymoon" period when the Communists appeared to grant freedom to Christians, all Catholic and Protestant institutions and churches were closed and many used for other purposes—with the exception of a few "showcase" churches in major cities. Soon all foreign missionaries were expelled from China.

With the mainland of China closed to foreign missionaries, OMS was nevertheless determined not to relinquish its call to minister to the people of China. The early 1950's marked the opening of two new fields among the Chinese—in Taiwan and Hong Kong.

With the reduction of tensions between China and the U.S. following Nixon's "ping pong diplomacy" has come fresh hope that the doors to China will again open. With travel restraints removed, many Christians travel freely in China. The persecuted church which some feared would die with the departure of missionaries has, on the contrary, become strong, vigorous, assuming at last a healthy national identity. The result has been a story of church growth unprecedented in the history of missions. A church of 2 million in 1949 has mushroomed into a great Christian community estimated today (1999) to number between 50 and 75 million. And this is but the beginning.

OMS has not forgotten China. For more than 20 years it sponsored a popular *Streams in the Desert* radio program, and now helps support national evangelists and seminaries within China and keeps the spiritual needs of China before its constituency.

Taiwan

At the 1950 OMS International Convention in Winona Lake, Indiana, Bob Pierce, founder of World Vision, described in dramatic fashion a recent conversation with President and Madame Chiang Kai Shek, now exiled on the island province of Taiwan. "Tell the Christians in America to help us," the Chiangs had urged Dr. Pierce. "Tell them to send us the Word of God for our 800,000 troops here on the island of Formosa. Come and bring the Gospel to these men."

The challenge resulted in the formation of a Gospel team headed by Dick Hillis (founder and president of Overseas Crusades) and OMS missionaries, Uri Chandler and Ellsworth Culver.

In the course of the team's ministry on Taiwan, Chandler came in contact with the Taiwan Holiness Church, a small but thriving association begun by OMS' Japanese Christians as a missionary effort in the early 1930's. (Although the people of Taiwan are Chinese, the island was a Japanese colony from 1895 until 1945.) Now Taiwan Holiness Church leaders were not slow to issue an invitation to OMS to send missionaries to their island to assist in church planting and the establishment of a Bible training center.

Veteran missionaries E.A. (Bud) Kilbourne and his wife, Hazel, were soon on their way. They were joined by their son, Elmer, and his wife Ella Ruth, and a contingent of "old China hands"—missionaries who had fled the China mainland during the Communist takeover. The party arrived in 1951 and, after considering several locations for the Bible school, finally decided on a choice property in Taichung, a large city in central Taiwan. The school was called the Central Taiwan Theological College. Today the Taiwan Holiness Church has some 90 congregations with about 10,000 members. The Central Taiwan Theological College has developed into a strong seminary with over 140 students.

OMS was one of the founding missions of Morrison Academy, an outstanding school for the education of missionary children in Asia. Our missionaries presently serve on the faculty and staff of the school.

Hong Kong

In 1954 OMS leaders in Los Angeles were startled by a request that came

came to them from an aging widow, then living in semi-retirement. Her name was Florence Munroe. For 40 years she and her husband had served in South China. Since her husband's recent death, she felt God compelling her to return to the people she so loved, many of whom were now refugees in Hong Kong.

For a widow nearing retirement age with no previous experience in field leadership or administration, to pioneer a new work in the swollen, problem-ridden colony of Hong Kong seemed foolhardy, to say the least. But Florence Munroe was not to be denied. After prayerful deliberation, the board gave their consent and "Auntie Mun" as she was affectionately known set sail, the first OMS appointee to Hong Kong.

The blessing of God was on her mission from the start. In a short time she had contacted a Chinese pastor trained in our Canton seminary, now a refugee in Hong Kong. With his help, a Gospel hall was opened. The establishment of churches and Sunday schools followed. Additional workers were added to keep pace with the rapid growth as believers were steadily added to the church.

In 1957 Auntie Mun was granted permission to utilize several large rooftops of huge refugee resettlement buildings (built in the shape of an H and hence dubbed H-blocks) for Christian schools. Other churches and missions followed suit. Thus began a remarkable educational and evangelistic ministry among the neglected refugee children of the colony. Later as the British government built regular elementary and secondary schools, the rooftop schools were phased out. In 1963, however, OMS obtained a choice property in Kowloon on which they erected Hong Kong Christian College (grades 1-12) and the sanctuary of Grace Church, the mother church of the denomination, designated Hong Kong Evangelical Church (HKEC).

Today HKEC has 18 organized churches with a membership in excess of 3,000. One of these is located in the former Portuguese colony of Macau.

India

Late in the summer of 1939, the OMS Board of Directors, at a meeting in Seoul, Korea, unanimously voted to open work in the vast subcontinent of India. Eugene Erny, at the time serving in north China, was their choice for the man to direct the new venture. Wesley and Betty Duewel and five other appointees from the U.S. joined him.

The missionary party at first located in Bangalore, South India. Hours were spent in prayer and consultation with other mission leaders, seeking God's guidance for the location of the new work. After a time they felt led to divide their forces and establish two centers. The first was opened in Allahabad in the north in 1942. The following year a second Bible school was started in the southern city of Gadag.

In the 1950's other areas were entered, one in Itarsi, mid-India, and another in the mountain district of Simla. Most significant, a seminary was opened in Madras under the direction of Garnett Philippe. This area was to prove exceedingly fruitful and continues to grow under the guidance of a dynamic Indian leader, Bishop Ezra Sargunum. Today India is the second largest OMS field, behind Korea. Organized churches number 1,152 with 980 additional preaching points. Total membership approaches 400,000. There are 72 ECC teams at work. In three seminaries and eleven Bible schools, some 830 students are in training for Christian ministry. Most heartening, almost all of the explosive growth has taken place during the last two decades when virtually all foreign missionaries have left India on account of government visa restrictions. Today only Graham and Carol Houghton remain. Graham is founder and director of an independent seminary in Bangalore, the South Asia Institute of Advanced Christian Studies (SAIACS).

Colombia

The very name of the mission, The Oriental Missionary Society[1], seemed to preclude the likelihood of opening work in non-Asian countries. Yet it happened in the manner already detailed in the story of Lettie Cowman. During the war years, when most of the Orient was inaccessible to foreign missionaries, OMS pursued its divine commission in Colombia, the "southland" which God had shown Mrs. Cowman in her hotel room in Winona Lake in 1942. A Bible training center was established in 1944 under the direction of B. H. Pearson and Bill Gillam. In 1951 local churches established by OMS were organized into the Association of Inter-American Evangelical Churches of Colombia.

To provide schooling for Protestant children, often denied an education in the Roman Catholic-administered public schools, the OMS churches established a number of Christian day schools. When graduates of these schools needed further education, OMS opened both high schools and a vocational training institute in Cristalina, a small town in an outlying area. Here, too, many young converts of the OMS riverboat ministry along the Magdalena waterway received schooling.

During the 1950's Colombia experienced a decade of violence known today as "La Violencia." Christian churches were attacked, pastors and believers persecuted, and at times killed. The legacy of those years continues in Colombia at this time, and it is unquestionably the most chronically violent country in the world. Yet the blood of the martyrs has proven to be the seed of the church. A large work has been opened in the capital city of Bogotá and an amazing evangelistic outreach exists within the national prisons where the drug dealers and hired assassins are incarcerated.

The association begun by OMS now has 120 congregations, while a network of churches more recently formed numbers 18 with about 2,200 members. Nine ECC teams are at work. There are 265 students enrolled in the seminary in Medellín.

Brazil

In the late 1940's Dr. George Ridout, a professor at Asbury College, made several evangelistic trips to Brazil. These brought him in contact with Reverend Jonathan Thomaz de Aquino, a national pastor. Ridout was so impressed with the zealous, Spirit-filled ministry of Reverend Aquino that he wrote OMS suggesting that the Society support him in his evangelistic work.

Thus, the first OMS contact was established with a field that would eventually prove most fruitful. The tie with Aquino eventuated in the conviction that the mission must enter Brazil—the largest country on the continent with a land area equal to that of the U.S. and a population then approaching 100 million.

In 1954 OMS opened a Bible seminary in Londrina in the state of Parana. A program of church planting in conjunction with the Brazil Every Creature Crusade followed this. Later, as the church grew, OMS outreach extended to Sao Paulo and Curitiba. Two church camps have also been exceedingly effective instruments for evangelism.

When OMS arrived in Brazil, our missionaries discovered Japanese churches, established years before and planted by the Japan Holiness Church. Through the years OMS has worked in close fellowship with these Japanese churches of OMS ancestry.

Presently The Missionary Church, founded by OMS, has 42 organized churches and 32 preaching points in Brazil with a membership of more than 6,300. The student body at the seminary numbers about 130.

Ecuador

In the early 1950's intensified persecution of Protestant churches in Colombia posed a growing threat to the continuance of foreign missionary presence in that land. In view of this, it seemed wise to establish a secondary base in an adjacent Spanish-speaking area, a base to which our missionaries could transfer should the government force the closedown of our work in Colombia. Ecuador was chosen for this purpose, and in 1952 OMS opened a center in Guayaquil, Ecuador's largest city. Although in God's providence missionaries were able to stay in Colombia, the work in Ecuador has continued, and other centers in Quito and Cuenca have been opened. A clinic and churches were also established in the upper Andes in an effort to reach the Saraguro Indians. In 1994 Good Shepherd Radio station was built to take the Gospel to these proud descendants of the once-mighty Inca nation.

In the late 1980's a large center was purchased in the heart of Guayaquil for an Encounter with God Church (designed to reach the city's middle and upper classes) and also a seminary.

Today the church founded by OMS has 28 organized churches and 17 preaching points with a membership of more the 4,000. At present 345 students are enrolled in seminary degree and certificate programs.

OMS also operated a dormitory for missionary children attending the Alliance Academy in Quito, an outstanding school for missionary children in Latin America.

Haiti

An unusual proposition made to the OMS Board of Directors in 1958 led to the mission's entering the field of Haiti. Radio station 4VEH in Cap Haitien, a work established by Mr. G.T. Bustin, was in a crisis. Funds were low and buildings were deteriorating. If OMS would pay a small mortgage that Bustin proposed, he would sign over the entire property and radio station to the Society.

OMS, however, was experiencing financial shortages of its own at this time. To enter a new field, some said, would be less than prudent. Nevertheless, after prayer and deliberation, Bustin's offer was accepted. Since then, Haiti has become one of the foremost fields of OMS activity. The all-but-defunct radio station has been renovated, new radio towers erected, and a powerful new transmitter installed, with pre-tuned radio sets placed in thousands of Haitian homes.

Along with the radio outreach has come a proliferation of other ministries—a vocational Bible institute, day schools, a medical/dental clinic, Every Creature Crusades and the planting of churches. A guest house and retreat center is operated by OMS in Port au Prince. The Cowman International School was also established to educate MKs and other English-speaking children in the Cap Haitien area.

Due to the proximity of Haiti to the U.S. mainland, thousands of laymen have visited the OMS work in Haiti on MFMI-sponsored work and witness crusades. As a result many of these have become missionaries or active in the support of missions.

Despite continuous political and social upheaval, the OMS ministry in Haiti continues to grow. Today there are two denominations founded by OMS: The Evangelical Church of Haiti has 52 congregations with 14,000 members and Evangelical Fellowship of Churches has 16 congregations with a membership of 2,513. About 100 students are presently enrolled in the Emmaus Bible School.

Indonesia

Indonesia, the former Dutch East Indies, is the largest Muslim nation in the world and the only one in which there is great responsiveness to the Gospel and a rapidly growing church. Following the abortive Communist coup in 1965, great numbers of Indonesians elected to become Christians. This presented unprecedented opportunities for missions in that land. OMS opened work in 1969 under the leadership of Dale McClain (formerly a missionary in China and Hong Kong) and Garry Parker. The city of Malang in East Java was chosen as the site for the OMS seminary and church headquarters. A second extension seminary was later opened in Central Java in the city of Salatiga. Despite Muslim opposition and political and economic turmoil, the work has continued to grow. At this time Nusantara Evangelical Church, founded by OMS, has 64 organized churches and 15 preaching points in Indonesia, with a membership of about 4,500. The two seminaries have a total of 140 students in both the degree and certificate programs.

Spain

With the end of the Francisco Franco dictatorship in 1969 dawned a new era of freedom for evangelicals in Spain. OMS opened work in the country in 1972 under the leadership of Burton Biddulph, formerly OMS field leader in Colombia.

A central church designated the Metropolitan Tabernacle was established in the capitol city of Madrid. At this time the Federation of Evangelical Churches, founded by OMS, has four churches with a combined membership of over 200. OMS co-operates with several other missions in The Evangelical Seminary of Madrid, which has about 100 students.

Philippines

Work in the Republic of the Philippines was begun in 1982 under the direction of Wesley Wildermuth, who had previously served as OMS field leader in both Japan and Indonesia. Home Bible studies in Metro Manila led to the establishment of Faith Fellowship Church in 1984 with William Oden as pastor. In time additional daughter churches were planted in the greater Manila area. This association of churches is called Faith Evangelical Church of the Philippines (FECP).

Faith Bible College, an institute to train pastors and Christian workers for the denomination, was established in 1991. It now has about 40 students.

In 1995 FECP began implementing the cell church strategy. At present there are more than 100 cell groups in seven established churches. Total membership is about 1000.

Russia

With the advent of Gorbachev's "glasnost" and "perestroika," leading to the collapse of the Soviet Union, a vast new door opened to evangelicals for ministry in Russia and much of Eastern Europe. Numerous government and educational leaders publicly bemoaned the fact that 70 years of atheistic Communism had left the nation without moral and ethical moorings. In an amazing and unprecedented move, Christians were invited to Russia to teach courses in ethics and morality, from a Christian perspective, in public schools.

In response, a coalition of more than 80 Christian organizations formed what they called The CoMission, committed to sending thousands of evangelical missionaries as well as quantities of Christian literature and films to Russia. OMS joined The CoMission and between 1992 and 1997 sent more than 250 short-term missionaries to Russia and other nations of the former Soviet Union. One of the most effective instruments for evangelism was the JESUS Film with a Russian soundtrack. The film was shown thousands of times in the nation's schools, public auditoriums and other venues.

As gradual opposition to the evangelical presence in public schools developed and opportunities for this kind of witness diminished, OMS began a transition to implement its four-fold strategy in Russia under the leadership of Harold Brown, formerly OMS field leader in Haiti. Today OMS has 17 Every Creature Crusade church-planting teams, five congregations, and the Moscow Evangelical Christian Seminary with 24 students. Two regional Bible schools have also been opened.

Hungary

In Hungary, as in Russia, the collapse of Communism signaled a new day of opportunity for missions in that country. Initially OMS and other mission groups were invited to assist the small evangelical denominations which had struggled to survive the long night of Communist suppression.

OMS entered Hungary in 1992 under the leadership of David Cosby, formerly an OMS missionary to Colombia. Missionaries of the Korean Evangelical Holiness Church soon joined it in partnership.

The mission center is located in Budapest. Although no churches have yet been planted nor a Bible seminary opened, missionaries are seeking to establish a beachhead through English evangelism ministries in public schools and youth camps. In addition two ECC teams presently work in Hungary.

Mexico

Although OMS was extensively involved in Every Creature Crusades in Mexico under the leadership of Lettie Cowman during the 1940's, no work was officially opened until 1990. In 1986 and 1987 OMS executives conducted surveys of Mexico, visiting possible sites for a new work and talking with a variety of mission leaders. As a result, in 1990 the board voted to officially open work in Mexico City under the direction of Max Edwards, formerly a missionary with OMS in Brazil.

From the start, the mission has implemented its historic four-fold strategy of Every Creature Crusades, church planting and training nationals in Bible training schools.

At this time OMS has three organized churches and two preaching points in Mexico with a total membership of 178. There are also eight ECC teams presently in the field. The Biblical Seminary of Mexico has over 50 students.

Mozambique

Although South Africa has long been an OMS sending country, it was not until 1994 that the Mission undertook the establishment of work on that great African continent. In this effort OMS South African Director, Alan Sylvester, particularly aided them. The task of leading the new field was given to Bruce Callendar, previously OMS field director in Ecuador.

At this point the first pioneer church plant is underway with attendance of 50, and plans are in place for aggressive church-planting evangelism both in the capitol, Maputo, and in the north. OMS has opened a school for missionary children and has plans for a seminary

Ireland

In 1996 the OMS Board of Trustees voted to open a work in Ireland. Summer evangelism teams began ministry in 1998. In 1999 Rev. Bill Oden, formerly OMS field director of the Philippines, was appointed as Ireland field director.

EVERY CREATURE CRUSADE EVANGELISM

In addition to the established OMS fields already listed, OMS through its ECC program, works in a number of other countries. These include Myanmar, Bangladesh, Kazakhstan, Estonia, Cuba, Dominican Republic, Venezuela, Nepal, Paraguay, Thailand and Vietnam. In these countries OMS works in association with its daughter churches or churches with compatible vision and doctrine. There are over 300 ECC teams presently working in 25 countries with over 1,000 evangelists.

MEN FOR MISSIONS INTERNATIONAL

Although churchwomen of every denomination have long been supporters of missionary endeavor, it was not until 1954 that the first men's missionary support group was formed.

God's instrument was a colorful evangelist named Dwight Ferguson from Mt. Gilead, Ohio. When OMS President Eugene Erny approached Ferguson about visiting OMS fields, the evangelist at first demurred. "Foreign missions is really not my thing," he explained. "God called me to preach the Gospel in the U.S." In the end, however, Ferguson reluctantly agreed to go, taking with him a friend, Stanley Tam, a businessman from Lima, Ohio. This historic journey deeply impacted both men and provided the inspiration for a new laymen's movement within OMS International.

At the OMS International Convention in Winona Lake that summer of 1954, on an impulse Ferguson rose to his feet to challenge men in the audience to radical involvement in foreign missions. "This is a job we have too long left to the ladies," he thundered. "Shame on us! It's time we got involved in the greatest task on earth!" The result was the formation of the "laymen's arm of OMS International," named Men For Missions. Later Men For Missions International (MFMI) councils were organized all over the U.S. and later in the British Isles, Australia, New Zealand and Canada. Under the auspices of MFMI, thousands of laymen have gone to mission fields on work and witness crusades. They have built churches, seminaries, camp facilities, missionary homes and roads. And wherever they have gone, they have shared their witness. Few of these laymen return from an MFM Crusade unchanged. Scores have given their lives to Christ for career missionary service.

The striking success of MFM inspired many similar organizations which have sprung up in both independent missions and mainline denominations.

Much of the success of Men For Missions must also be attributed to the zealous and energetic leadership of MFM Executives Larry and Harry Burr and Warren Hardig.

SENDING COUNTRIES

Although OMS was in the beginning an American mission, the Cowmans very early attracted supporters in the British Isles, most notable of whom was Oswald Chambers, who visited the mission while in Japan. One of the earliest missionaries to Korea was a distinguished Welsh evangelist, John Thomas. Following Charles' death, Lettie's writings and Every Creature Crusade activity won thousands of friends and a great OMS family of supporters around the world. The great popularity of *Streams in the Desert* in particular was used of God to familiarize millions with the work of OMS.

In the early 1950's co-operating countries were designated OMS sending countries and mission offices with national directors opened. These sending countries are: The United States, the British Isles, including Scotland and North Ireland, Canada, Australia, New Zealand and South Africa.

SHORT-TERM MISSIONARIES

Following World War II with the advent of speedy, safe and economical air travel on a global scale, missions began sending great numbers of young people overseas for summer assignments. In the 1950's OMS created NOW Corps (Novice Overseas Witness) to recruit and send collegians to mission fields for terms of service from periods of two weeks to several months. To this, later was added the M-1 and M-2 programs which provide overseas service opportunities for terms of one to two years. NOW Corps is now called International Link.

Today more than one-half of all OMS missionaries attribute their decisions to become career missionaries to a short-term experience on a mission field.

[1]The name of the mission was officially changed from The Oriental Missionary Society to OMS International in 1971.